# THE
# AZTEC,
# INCA & MAYA
# EMPIRES

D1561188

# THE
# AZTEC, INCA & MAYA EMPIRES

## The Illustrated History of the Ancient Peoples of Mesoamerica & South America

MARTIN J. DOUGHERTY

amber
BOOKS

© 2018 Amber Books Ltd

All rights reserved. No part of this publication may be reproduced, stored in a retrieval system, or transmitted in any form or by any means, electronic, mechanical, photocopying, recording, or otherwise, without prior written permission of the copyright holder.

Published by
Amber Books Ltd
United House
North Road
London
N7 9DP
United Kingdom
www.amberbooks.co.uk
Instagram: amberbooksltd
Facebook: www.facebook.com/amberbooks
Twitter: @amberbooks

ISBN: 978-1-78274-679-9

Project Editor: Sarah Uttridge
Designer: Jerry Williams
Picture Research: Terry Forshaw

Printed in Italy

# Contents

# Introduction

The 'cradle of civilization' is generally thought of as being the Fertile Crescent of ancient Mesopotamia and Egypt, a region that gave rise to a number of civilizations over the centuries. These may have influenced one another during their early development and in many cases interacted.

SOMETIMES THESE interactions were violent and sometimes they were through trade and the exchange of ideas. Other civilizations grew up in the river valleys of India and China, and may or may not have had contact with one another. Exactly how to define 'civilization' is a difficult question, but as a general rule a candidate for the title will display certain hallmarks. Urbanization, social organization, agriculture and art are generally considered to be indicators of a civilization rather than what might be called a 'complex culture'. Thus, some quite advanced societies are not described as civilizations as they do not quite fit the standard definition.

At first glance, it may seem that the factors defining a civilization are interdependent. The large-scale production of food required to support an urbanized population depends upon a degree of social organization, as does the capability to get the

OPPOSITE: The degree of organization required to build great structures such as those at Chichen Itza is one of the hallmarks of civilization, but not all of the great builder-cultures were true civilizations.

food to where it is needed and to store it until required. It might seem, therefore, that all civilizations would be very similar, and in many cases this is true. However, the early civilizations of the Americas challenge this assumption.

The earliest known large-scale settlements – 'proto-cities' – developed in the Middle East. Jericho, the oldest of them all, grew up as a series of settlements in the Neolithic (late Stone Age) and Chalcolithic (the short Copper Age preceding the introduction of bronze-working) eras. Exactly when it became something that would be considered a city is open to debate, but by 7500 BC or so other proto-cities existed in the Middle East and the development of civilization could be said to be underway.

The first society to fit the standard definition of a civilization appeared in Mesopotamia around 3500 BC, probably as the result of a steady trend towards urbanization and centralized power. Civilization is known to have existed along the Nile

BELOW: **A modern reconstruction of the geology of the Valley of Mexico. Lying high above sea level and surrounded by mountains, the valley was a 'cradle of civilization' in the Americas.**

by 3100 BC and in the Indus Valley by 2600 BC. China had developed a civilization by 1600 BC.

Some of these civilizations had contact with one another, and it is possible that ideas were carried by traders or wanderers, gradually spreading across the land from the Middle East to China. There is little chance that the same happened across the Atlantic or Pacific oceans to the Americas of that era. The Beringia land bridge was long gone by the rise of the first cities, submerged by rising sea levels. Craft capable of navigating the open sea, let alone the vast expanse of an ocean, were not available to the earliest civilizations of the Fertile Crescent, India or China.

> The great American cultures stand as proof that there is not just one way to create a civilization.

Thus the rise of the earliest known civilization in the Americas, dating from 2600 BC or so, must have occurred independently. This culture, known to us as the Maya civilization, developed without the influence of other civilizations but not in complete isolation. It was shaped by the unique environment of the Americas and the advanced cultures that had gone before it.

The Maya and the other Central and South American cultures that came after them existed in a very different environment to those of the rest of the world. There were no horses in the Americas, which were fundamental elsewhere, were not developed. The great American cultures stand as proof that there is not just one way to create a civilization.

## THE AMERICAS IN THE DISTANT PAST

South America is an ancient continent, isolated for most of its existence. Stable rock formations known as cratons form the framework of the landmass. These have existed since the end of the Precambrian era around 451 million years ago, and are probably much older. Along with later accreted material, these cratons were part of the ancient supercontinent Gondwanaland, which collided with Earth's other supercontinent, Laurasia, to form a single landmass known as Pangaea.

ABOVE: **Rock art at La Lindosa in Colombia may date from as early as 10,000 BC. The images may have been intended to educate younger generations, or may have had mystical significance to their creators.**

Pangaea is thought to have contained all of Earth's land until it began to break up around 200 million years ago. About 180 million years ago, what are now Africa and South America broke away from Gondwanaland; around 40 million years after that they separated. The space between them formed the Atlantic Ocean. Up until this point, plants and animals could spread from other regions into what is now South America, but once the seas opened up, the ecosystems of the different continents evolved in their own way. This had significant implications for the development of civilization in the Americas when humans finally arrived.

South America was isolated from all other continents until around three million years ago, when it was joined to the North

American continent by the Panama Isthmus. This was likely the result of plate tectonics; a drifting together of landmasses that created a bridge between the northern and southern Americas. Since this time, species have been able to move back and forth. The northern portion of the isthmus was probably part of North America; its fossil record holds similar species.

Continental drift and the collision of rock masses are partially responsible for the geography of modern South America. Volcanism, plate collisions and subduction resulted in the creation of the Andes mountain range, running almost the entire length of the continent. The mountain chain is made up of several ranges with high plateaux and some lower-lying areas, but on the whole creating a major barrier to movement across the continent.

The narrow coastal plain west of the Andes has a varied climate. Some areas receive enormous amounts of rainfall; others almost none. Those regions with enough water are extremely fertile. To the east of the Andes, the northern part of the continent is dominated by the Amazon basin, with its dense rainforests, while the south has extensive plains.

Perhaps as much as nine million years ago, the extensive glaciation that would cover much of Earth's surface was beginning in the southern Andes. Glaciation reached its maximum extent around a million years ago. As elsewhere, the 'ice age' in South America was characterized by retreats and new advances of the ice until around 12,000 years ago, when the climate began to warm rapidly. As the ice retreated, the modern flora and fauna of South America began to emerge.

BELOW: **The Guilá Naquitz Cave near Mitla in Mexico was inhabited for several periods around 9–10,000 years ago, and again much later. Along with cave art, these early people left behind evidence demonstrating the beginnings of domestication of some plant species.**

## FLORA AND FAUNA OF SOUTH AND CENTRAL AMERICA

By the time humans entered the Americas, unique ecosystems had developed on the two American continents and the isthmus between them. Plant and animal species had developed in isolation up until the land bridge was established, but after this migration began to take place. A period known as the Great American Interchange saw species moving both ways and in some cases adapting to their new environment.

Some species, such as the horse, were not present at all in the Americas and were not available to humans when they arrived. The domestication of the horse for warfare and labour was an enormous influence on the development of civilization elsewhere; without it, the people of the Americas found different solutions to the same challenges.

As the climate warmed, the terrain changed. New lands opened up as the ice retreated; they were claimed first by plants, then by animals feeding off them. Human hunters would eventually follow these invaders into the new territories. Around this time, about 12,000 years ago, many of the megafauna species became extinct. It is generally believed that human hunters were one of the factors that drove mammoth and

RIGHT: Although it is not possible to say for certain whether humans drove large animals such as the giant tapir to extinction, the discovery of bones – often with weapon or tool marks – at inhabited sites suggests that hunting was a factor.

mastodon to extinction in North America, though climate change
and the loss of their habitat as the flora of the region responded
was also important.

Among the species encountered by early humans entering
the Americas was the glyptodont, a large armoured herbivore
with a spiked tail. The glyptodont evolved in an era when South
America was dominated by giant carnivorous birds, although
these were long extinct. Although undoubtedly difficult prey,
glyptodont were hunted by humans and their shells used to
make tools.

Like other megafauna, the glyptodont became extinct not long
after humans spread through the Americas, although smaller
relatives such as the armadillo survived. Some of the large
creatures of the Americas survived in refuges such as islands
or very remote areas, almost to recent times. The giant sloth

ABOVE: Increasingly
advanced tools and
weapons enabled humans
to tame their environment
and cooperatively take
very large prey. This trend
would ultimately lead to
the rise of civilization.

ABOVE: The glyptodont was a remnant of an earlier age, and represented a difficult challenge for early hunters. It is thought that glyptodont shells were used as ready-made shelters by early hunters.

survived on Caribbean islands until humans arrived there perhaps 5–7000 years ago.

Whether or not humans were responsible for the extinction of the largest land animals in the southern Americas, their demise left the region without animals that would be suitable for labour. There were plenty of edible species to be hunted, including turkey and deer, but the early human inhabitants of the Americas were largely forced to rely on their own muscles rather than those of animals.

### EARLIEST HUMAN HABITATION

There is no clear evidence of human habitation in South or Central America before the Last Glacial Maximum around 30,000 years ago. Controversial claims have been made, based upon artefacts dated to a much earlier period, but this dating process is considered questionable by much of the scientific community.

The commonly accepted model of human settlement in the Americas is of tribes wandering across the land bridge of Beringia (the modern Aleutian Islands and Bering Strait) from Asia into North America. This took place over a period of several thousand years, and was made possible by lower sea levels during the Ice Age. As the ice retreated and fertile land opened up, sea levels also rose and eventually isolated the Americas from Asia.

There is solid evidence that humans had reached what is now New Mexico around 12–13,000 years ago. The traditional theory that these people moved through an ice-free corridor east of the Rocky Mountains has been questioned in recent years. It is now thought that humans spread down the Pacific coast as well as or instead of moving through the interior.

Humans continued to spread eastwards across the North American continent as the ice retreated. Movement southwards was facilitated by the fertile conditions of the Pacific coast, and would have enabled groups of nomadic hunter-gatherers to travel down the Panama Isthmus and into South America. There, coastal movement was probably much easier than going inland; the Andes would have channelled early expansion either south through what is now Peru or along the northern coast of the continent.

As the early humans moved throughout their new continent, they would encounter different terrain and conditions that required changes to their lifestyle. New skills were needed to survive in the high plateaux or the rainforests, whereas the familiar coastal terrain offered greater certainty of success. Those groups that went east and migrated into the Amazonian rainforest found a land that could support them once they learned its ways, but it was not an environment that was conducive to the development of great civilizations.

BELOW: The jaguar was significant to several Mesoamerican cultures, representing power and majesty as well as the ability to see the future or into the hearts of people. Images with both human and jaguar features may represent a spiritual or physical transformation.

# OTHER SETTLEMENT THEORIES

IT HAS BEEN SUGGESTED – with some supporting evidence – that the Pacific coast of South America was settled by early mariners who established communities in suitable places and then spread northwards. This is plausible, especially since some archaeological finds have been dated to 18,500 years before the present. People in Asia were building boats around this time and could have followed the coasts all the way to South America.

There have also been suggestions that Polynesian islanders travelled vast distances across the Pacific to settle in South America. Such a voyage is possible in an ocean-going canoe – though it is a terrifyingly risky prospect – and there is evidence of contact between the remote Pacific islanders and people from South America long before Europeans arrived in the region. However, it is more commonly thought that the contact was the other way around – mariners from South America visited the Polynesians.

There is much conflicting evidence, and many interpretations are possible. It is possible that humans took multiple routes into Central and South America. The 'coastal migration' model provides the simplest explanation, however, and when considering the movement of groups of people with all their belongings, tools, infants and young children, 'simple' equates to 'most likely'.

BELOW: Hundreds of petroglyphs were discovered at Toro Muerto in Peru, dating back to the Wari culture of 500–1000 AD.

Thus, the people of the rainforests went their own way, developing a culture that was sophisticated and successful even if it did not meet the definition of 'civilization' as used by Europeans. Those that remained west of the Andes, and the people of the Central American Isthmus, on the other hand, produced a series of civilizations to rival anything that ever emerged in Europe.

## THE RISE OF CIVILIZATION IN SOUTH AMERICA

For many centuries after the settlement of the Americas, humans lived a nomadic or semi-nomadic life supported by the hunting and gathering of food. The society of these people was undoubtedly sophisticated, with social norms, rules that were as binding as any law, and oral traditions dating back many generations. These wandering bands produced art, mainly petroglyphs produced by laboriously pecking at a large rock with a smaller one. Their culture may have been quite advanced, but it was not what we define as a civilization.

> There is a limit to how large a hunter-gatherer band can grow, although this depends greatly upon local conditions.

There is a limit to how large a hunter-gatherer band can grow, although this depends greatly upon local conditions. In times of plenty, bands might gather together and, in some regions – notably the Mississippi valley of North America – have undertaken great works such as the construction of mound complexes. The ability to carry out large building projects pushes the boundaries of what is considered a civilization, and although they are often called 'mound cities', many of these structures were used for purposes other than dwelling.

The move from a nomadic hunter-gatherer lifestyle to a sedentary one based upon agriculture was by no means inevitable, but it was more or less essential to the development of what we call civilization. The rich fisheries of the Pacific coast were able to support a large static population, but inland it was necessary to cultivate food in order to make large villages and towns viable. Once this move to a more sedentary lifestyle

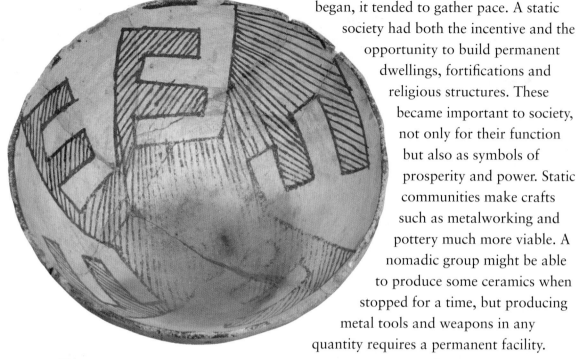

began, it tended to gather pace. A static society had both the incentive and the opportunity to build permanent dwellings, fortifications and religious structures. These became important to society, not only for their function but also as symbols of prosperity and power. Static communities make crafts such as metalworking and pottery much more viable. A nomadic group might be able to produce some ceramics when stopped for a time, but producing metal tools and weapons in any quantity requires a permanent facility.

ABOVE: This pottery bowl, produced by the Anasazi people of North America, demonstrates a common trait among early cultures – the desire to make objects more than merely functional by adding decoration or meaningful images.

## CERAMICS AND METALWARE

Without ceramics or metalware, some activities are very difficult to carry out. The making of stew, for example, requires a dish or pot of some kind. Humble as it might be, stew is one of the staples of human endeavour. It can be put together out of almost anything edible, and enables use to be made of foods that have only a marginal value.

Other methods are possible, but a ceramic or metal pot enables a stew to be kept 'on the go' more or less permanently. Additional ingredients are added over time, ensuring that there is always food of decent quality available. For workers who eat when they have finished their tasks rather than being presented with a meal at a set time, the stewpot is of great importance.

Various preceramic cultures have been identified in South America dating back 15,000 years. A find at Lake Lauricocha gives its name to the 'Lauricocha culture', although it is unlikely that this was an organized society in any real sense. The Lauricocha culture essentially comprised numerous bands of hunter-gatherers whose lifestyle would be similar out of necessity.

The Lauricocha culture produced well-made bone and stone tools, and created art in the form of cave paintings. They also appear to have practised sacred rituals, including funerary rites. The Lauricocha culture is considered to have existed, in gradually evolving form, from around 8000 BC to 2500 BC. By the end of this period, the production of ceramics was becoming widespread.

Ceramics are known to have been produced in the Amazon basin since 3000 BC, and quite possibly much earlier. Ceramic vessels were produced in northern South America as early as 2500 BC or perhaps earlier, with the techniques spreading up the Panama Isthmus northwards. By 1600 BC, the firing of ceramic vessels was commonplace throughout Mesoamerica and into what is now New Mexico.

Metalworking began with gold and copper, both of which can be extracted in their natural state without a need for chemical processes or heating to free them from the surrounding rock. Gold and copper can also be worked without heating. Gold items have been found in South America dating from around 2000 BC, and copper items from 1500 BC. However, there is some evidence that copper was being worked earlier and may have been subject to heating during the process.

Metals were not used to make tools and weapons as commonly as in other cultures. Instead, metal items were produced for decorative and ceremonial purposes. Similarly, civilization in South and Central America developed without many of the technological advances found elsewhere. The wheel, for example, was not put to any practical application, although rollers were used to assist in moving large loads such as stone blocks. Wheeled toys have been found in Central

BELOW: A Mayan vessel found at Kaminaljuyu in Guatemala. It is designed to stand on its own built-in tripod, perhaps over a fire. As with many such objects, functional components such as the lid handle are intricately decorated.

America, but there is no evidence of wheels being implemented as a vehicle component. One possible reason for this is the lack of suitable animals to pull such a conveyance. Lacking horses, the South American cultures had little incentive to build chariots or carts; in many areas, the terrain was unsuitable in any case.

# ERAS AND STAGES IN CENTRAL AND SOUTHERN AMERICA

THE PREHISTORY OF SOUTHERN and Central America is commonly divided into several stages, which roughly correspond to technological and social developments. Any such classification is a generalization at best, of course, since local variations will always exist.

*The Lithic Stage* begins with the first known presence of humans in the Americas. The term Paleo-Indian is also used for this era. Tools were of stone or bone, and society was based on hunter-gatherer bands.

*The Archaic Stage* began around 8000 BC and was characterized by a move away from big game hunting to a more diversified gathering of resources. Deliberate cultivation of food crops began, but large-scale agriculture was yet to be developed.

*The Formative Stage* generally began around 1000 BC and was characterized by a move towards a settled lifestyle based on small-scale agriculture. 'Pre-Classic' and 'Neo-Indian' are alternative terms. Cultures of this era generally began to develop a hierarchical society led by warriors or religious figures and possessed technologies such as making pottery and weaving cloth.

*The Classic Stage* refers to advanced cultures. Those that achieved this stage did so between 200 and 1200 AD.

*The Post-Classic Stage* refers to the most developed form of the civilizations that existed when Europeans first entered the Americas. 'Later Prehispanic' is an alternative term, referring to the last years before contact with European – notably Spanish – explorers.

The general term for the era before European contact is pre-Columbian, which recognizes the enormous changes wrought by European contact. On a more local scale, it is often useful to consider the development of civilization in terms of 'horizons' (periods of stability in which civilizations developed and flourished) with intermediate periods between where there was no large-scale civilization or advanced culture in that region.

The construction of public buildings, one of the hallmarks of civilization, normally follows the development of metalworking, ceramics and other enabling technologies. Yet in South America there is evidence of great works predating these developments. The oldest ruins found at Sechin Bajo have been dated to around 3500 BC, along with later structures. These form part of a group of ancient ruins found in the area of the Sechin valley. If the dating is confirmed, these will be the oldest known large-scale constructions in South America.

The culture of the Sechin valley survived and developed for many centuries, although some of its centres appear to have been abandoned. The site at Cerro Sechin, notable for its friezes depicting warfare and conquest, was abandoned in around 800 BC. Other construction took place later, such as what initially appeared to be a fortress at Chankillo.

The Chankillo site, with many gates and 13 towers, was initially believed to be a fortification of some kind; perhaps a palace. It is now thought to be a highly advanced astronomical installation used to calculate the timings of solstices and other important dates. If this is correct, Chankillo is the oldest such site in the Americas.

The people who built these structures are often referred to as the Casma/Sechin culture after the river valleys they inhabited, but this is not considered to be a civilization as such. Other proto-civilizations would arise before the first true civilizations (by the standard definition) flowered in South and Central America.

ABOVE: **Although referred to as masks, the stone faces associated with Teotihuacan were clearly not intended to be worn as they are heavy and lack eyeholes. They represent a generic face lacking distinguishing features.**

# CHAPTER 1

# Complex Cultures in South America

Civilization, as we define it, did not develop overnight. Several cultures arose that could be considered 'civilized' but that lacked some of the defining features of a civilization, such as particular technologies or centralized authority.

THESE PROTO-CIVILIZATIONS are generally referred to as 'complex cultures'. The earliest known civilization, in the Americas was in the region now known as Norte Chico, on the coast of Peru. The region is dry but receives sufficient water to support a population as a result of maritime precipitation and rivers flowing down from the Andes to the east. There is some debate as to whether Norte Chico qualifies as a civilization as such, as some of its hallmarks are missing, but the ability to construct large building complexes and to support an advanced society puts this culture at least on the fringe of civilization. There is evidence of human habitation in the area as early as 9000 BC, although this is a population concentration

OPPOSITE: The construction of monumental buildings like the La Huanaca pyramid is one of the hallmarks of civilization, indicating not merely capability but also aspirations beyond the mundane needs of survival.

ABOVE: The majority of the population of Caral-Supe were farmers, dwelling in well-planned housing complexes. The city's elite lived closer to the pyramid complex in the centre of the city.

rather than a civilization. Over time, the population expanded and several centres began to develop. Some of these lay on the coast; others inland. At one time, it was thought that population centres developed first along the coast where they could be supported by fishing and similar activities, but it appears that these centres grew at approximately the same rate regardless of their location, suggesting that development was less focused.

The development of the Norte Chico civilization may have been made possible by trade between the population centres. Those inland produced cotton, which was traded for fish caught using the nets made from it. Although this culture did not produce art that has survived, its people undertook great building works. The most notable of these are at Caral, in the Supe valley, where six ceremonial pyramids, along with other structures, survive there to this day.

Along with the pyramids, the Norte Chico people also built irrigation canals and presumably practised agriculture. There is debate about how urbanized the population was, however. Urbanization, along with art expression, is a hallmark of civilization; without it, Norte Chico is sometimes considered an advanced complex culture rather than a true civilization.

Norte Chico could be thought of as a proto-civilization, emerging at a time when the very concept of civilization was completely new. The first city-states began to appear in Mesopotamia in 5000–3500 BC, and the earliest evidence of cities in South America has been dated to 3500–3000 BC. There was no direct connection between these two emerging cultures, of course, but the apparent synchronicity may not be mere coincidence. The changing climate resulting from the end of the Ice Age made population growth and the eventual rise of cities possible, but this warming was interrupted by periods of return to much colder conditions. The last of these, the Younger Dryas, is thought to have ended around 11,700 years ago in the northern hemisphere.

This period was characterized by warming in some parts of the southern hemisphere, but the overall effect was one of abrupt climate change that would have disrupted the growth

BELOW: The layout of Caral-Supe indicates city planning and a high degree of organization. It housed more than 3000 people at a time when the very concept of a city was new.

of populations and the rise of complex societies. The earliest known habitation at Norte Chico occurs a few hundred years after the end of the Younger Dryas, at a time of relative climatic stability. Thus, the conditions were right for the rise of urbanized populations and, eventually, civilization.

The Norte Chico pyramid sites are notable for their lack of evidence of violence. No weapons or evidence of their use such as skeletons with injuries have been found, and there is no indication of fortification. This does not mean that conflict did not occur, of course, and it may be that the pyramid sites were sacred and thus off-limits for fighting. It is equally possible that the Norte Chico people were peaceable and had little need for conflict.

The site at Caral has been described as the oldest urban site in the Americas, although this claim has been challenged. It is thought that its stepped pyramids were constructed by filling reed bags with rocks and using these as building blocks. Carbon-dating of the remains of these bags has allowed the construction of the main pyramid at Caral to be dated to around 2600 BC.

> The Norte Chico culture was highly influential on the development of South American civilizations.

RIGHT: Archaeologists have discovered many bone flutes in the ruins of Caral, suggesting a love of music which in turn implies this was an advanced and accomplished culture even if it did not fit the formal definition of a civilization.

The pyramid was later enlarged and remodelled (around 2200 BC).

The Norte Chico civilization developed into its final form after 3500 BC, which is also the earliest date postulated for the building of true cities in the region. At this time, the population balance seems to have moved inland, with coastal communities becoming smaller and inland centres being enlarged.

ABOVE: Bags woven from plant fibres were used for many purposes, from construction to fishing. There is evidence that inland cities traded cotton products for seafood from the coast.

Caral and other Norte Chico sites went into decline around 1800 BC. It is not clear why, but there is some evidence that the population migrated to other parts of what is now Peru. Irrigation canals in more fertile lands to the north have been dated to a period corresponding to this decline, so it is possible that the people were lured away by opportunities elsewhere.

The Norte Chico culture was highly influential on the development of South American civilization. Not only did its people take away their skills at building large structures and irrigation canals, but other concepts seem to have developed there as well. A quipu (a device for keeping records using knotted cords) was found at Caral. Similar devices were used by later South American cultures, notably the Inca. Music was an important part of the culture; numerous carved flutes have been found at Norte Chico sites.

Little is known about the politics of the people of Norte Chico, but they may have practised gender equality. A female burial dating from around 4500 years ago included valuable goods indicating a status as high as any man of the same society. There is little evidence of human sacrifice as practised elsewhere.

Although they made many advances, the people of Norte Chico did not have pottery. This is unusual; most societies

# MONUMENTAL ARCHITECTURE IN THE AMERICAS

EARLY CULTURES IN THE Americas built mound complexes, typically of earth, which were developed into the characteristic stepped pyramids by the great civilizations of South and Central America. These were temples, but since political and religious leadership were intertwined they also served as centres for administration and political authority.

The earliest known pyramids in the Americas have been dated to around 2600 BC, and many were remodelled or rebuilt several times. This was not mere whim, although there was an element of self-glorification by rulers who ordered such great works. The modification and renewal of the pyramid was part of its function, maintaining a constant reconnection to the gods through planning and labour.

Pyramids were constructed of adobe bricks, dressed stone or reed bags

ABOVE: Sambaquis, or shell mounds, were thought to be refuse piles rather than deliberate constructions. Burial sites nearby suggest a ceremonial function.

containing smaller rocks, which were used as building blocks. The remains of these bags have enabled some pyramids to be carbon-dated, whereas a purely stone construction would be far more difficult to date accurately.

Pyramid-shaped structures found in Brazil have been dated to 3000 BC or so, which would make them the oldest in the world if they were accepted as being pyramids in the same sense as those found elsewhere. However, the Brazilian pyramids are constructed of seashells rather than masonry and were for many years assumed to be refuse piles rather than deliberate monumental structures.

developed the ability to cast pots of clay before becoming able to build large structures, but no evidence has been found that the Norte Chico culture developed this technology at all. Gourds were used for storage and were in some cases decorated with the few examples of art to be found.

It seems likely that the trade network of the Norte Chico people went far beyond trading fish and cotton among their own communities. One of the few pieces of art ever found depicts a monkey; grave goods carved in the shape of jungle animals have also been unearthed. This suggests that the Norte Chico culture had contact with people on the far side of the Andes. Coastal trade would also have enabled the people of Norte Chico to spread their ideas among other emerging cultures even before their own society went into decline and the population began to move away.

## THE EARLY HORIZON

There is no indication that the Norte Chico civilization was an empire or even a centralized state of any sort. It appears to have been a decentralized culture whose people shared common practices and social values. After the decline of the Norte Chico

BELOW: The Chávin culture is named for the primary archaeological site associated with it; Chavín de Huantar. It is not known what the people of the region called themselves or their society as they left no written records.

BELOW: Little art survives from the Chavín culture. What does exist often depicts half-human, half-animal figures which may represent priests taking on the form of other creatures, either spiritually or literally.

civilization, these values would have spread wherever people went, but for several centuries there was no culture in Peru with the hallmarks of a civilization.

The Chavín culture, named for the archaeological site at Chavín de Huántar, appears to have emerged around 1000 BC, although archaeological finds suggest a period of development beginning well before that. The Chavín culture is generally considered to define the Early Horizon of civilization in Peru.

Little is known about the rise of the culture, although it appears to have been led by religious figures with little evidence

of military activity or violence of any sort. It may be that there was no real need or opportunity for conflict, with plenty of resources to support the limited population and significant terrain barriers making warfare difficult.

A number of religious structures have been found predating the Chavín culture but sharing some characteristics. The first of these was at Kotosh, resulting in these structures and their associated beliefs being labelled the Kotosh Tradition. The Kotosh Tradition followed on from earlier religious cultures in the same region, and forms part of the Late Preceramic era of development in Peru.

> The Chavín people domesticated animals and practised agriculture in addition to fishing in the rivers of the region.

By the rise of the Chavín culture, pottery and metalworking had been implemented on a large scale, and the social order seems to have been well established. A priestly or shamanistic caste were the social elite, with higher-status citizens living close to the main religious sites. These took the form of monumental buildings of stone and of highly sophisticated design. The housing of religious centres within walled buildings to which access was limited suggests that religion was the source of power within Chavín society and that the elite were careful to control access to it.

It is thought that Chavín religious practices may have involved the use of psychotropic drugs. Their art depicts strange creatures that seem to be part human and part animal, bird or crocodile. It may be that the use of psychotropics was reserved for the shaman caste or the upper echelons of society, and that the connection this created with the supernatural world was a symbol of or a reward for status in society. However, it is not certain that drugs were used. Equipment for producing suitable substances has been found and some Chavín art certainly looks as if it was created under the influence of drugs, but nothing can be said for certain.

The Chavín people domesticated animals and practised agriculture in addition to fishing in the rivers of the region. Their culture continued to develop over time, but around 300 BC a decline began. The reasons for this are not clear, but it has been

BELOW: The Moche culture produced intricate pottery, notably jugs, depicting various aspects of life. Crafts such as weaving are common along with sexual themes and, as in this case, sacrifice.

hypothesized that trade between the centres of Chavín culture was greatly reduced.

The Chavín civilization depended on close contact not only for the usual economic reasons but also for social control. Their religion was the factor that bound society together and this required regular reinforcement. Without it, communities gradually drifted away. The eclipse of the Chavín culture was complete by around 200 AD, after which, what is generally referred to as the Early Intermediate period began.

## EARLY INTERMEDIATE CULTURES

During the Early Intermediate period, technology continued to advance in Peru, with improvements in metalworking and pottery. There was no single dominant society at the time, but both the Moche and Nazca cultures were important in their own area.

The Moche culture was decentralized and could not be considered to be a state or unified political entity. Instead it was a confederation of generally like-minded people who spoke two different (but related) languages and had distinct artistic traditions.

The Moche culture began to emerge around 1 AD and centred on the Chicama and Trujillo valleys in northern Peru. The Moche people were adept builders and skilled agriculturalists who built irrigation systems to support their crops. They were also more warlike than the Chavín culture, and appear to have spread their power through conquest.

The Moche culture built pyramids, like many other groups in the region. The two pyramids at their capital, known as Moche, were apparently used as mausoleums and for ceremonies. They were decorated with art depicting

religious scenes; from these, it is known that the Moche had a sky god and a moon goddess.

These appear to have been fearsome gods, to be propitiated rather than adored. The Moche practised human sacrifice, using prisoners taken in war as well as members of Moche society. The victims were mutilated, their blood placed in goblets as an offering to the gods, and their bodies hurled from the pyramid. There is some evidence that sacrifices were made to appease the gods in times of flooding or other environmental hardships – a practice not uncommon in early civilizations.

The Moche culture declined from the 500s, possibly as a result of environmental changes. Sand from the coast was deposited by wind in quantities that choked the irrigation canals and made clearance difficult. The expanding Wari culture may also have begun to apply pressure on the Moche.

Whatever the cause, the population began to relocate elsewhere. A large migration north to the Lambayeque Valley appears to have resulted in the rise of a new culture there.

The Nazca culture, centred on Cahuachi, was also decentralized, with large-scale action characterized by cooperation at need rather than formal authority. The Nazca culture followed on from the Paracas culture, which existed from around 800 BC in the same general area. The Paracas people

ABOVE: The Moche pyramid at Huaca del Sol was built of adobe bricks. Construction took place over at least eight distinct phases. Continual rebuilding and improvement of monumental structures was a common practice among South American civilizations.

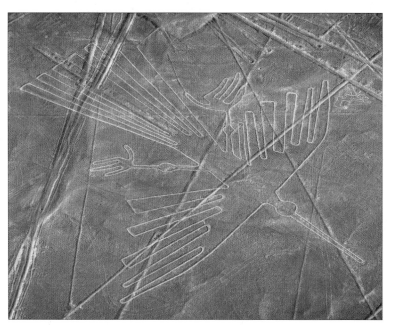

ABOVE: **The Nazca Lines were created by removing the dark surface layer and exposing the lighter stone underneath. Around 700 geoglyphs exist; some, like the Condor, are complex whilst others are simply geometrical shapes.**

created geoglyphs – large designs marked out on the ground – which may have inspired the later Nazca people to do the same. Paracas geoglyphs differ from those of the Nazca people however, both in terms of location and what they depict.

From around 150 AD, the Paracas people shared their lands with the Topara culture, whose members appear to have migrated southwards into Paracas lands. There is little evidence of conflict, and the melding of the two cultures was a strong influence on the emerging Nazca.

The Nazca people were skilled at finding water in an otherwise arid land, and at directing it to where it was needed. It was the dryness of their environment that enabled the Nazca's greatest creations, the so-called Nazca Lines, to survive to the present day. The lines are geoglyphs depicting animals and birds as well as geometric designs, and are so large in scale that they can only be appreciated from the air.

This, along with some creative interpretation of the designs, has given rise to a number of imaginative claims about the meaning of the Nazca Lines. Most famously, it has been claimed that the lines were inscribed by space travellers. Other, perhaps more credible, theories suggest that the lines were created as a sort of calendar used to calculate solstices and other important annual events, or that they had religious significance in ensuring good rainfall or the continuance of other water sources.

The same designs depicted on the Nazca Lines are repeated in their pottery; they also wove complex textiles. The Nazca made use of wool from llamas and other animals that live in the highlands, far from their coastal valley homes, and feathers from birds whose habitats were equally distant. It is clear that they traded for these goods, perhaps using their pottery and textiles.

Their pottery was finely made and decorated in a style that evolved over time. In addition to portrayals of ritual and images of creatures, Nazca pottery was also decorated in an abstract manner that often made use of the shape of the vessel. The Nazca were skilled goldsmiths, creating ceremonial masks as well as other decorations for the face and head that may have had a ritual function.

The Nazca appear to have had a shamanistic religion, using psychotropic drugs to communicate with other worlds. There appears to be an element of transformation about their rituals,

BELOW: There is some debate about what Nazca masks signify. This funerary mask is likely to be a depiction of the sun, a common theme in South American religion, but other interpretations are possible.

# PYRAMID THEORIES

THE FACT THAT ANCIENT cultures in widely separated areas – Egypt, South America and Asia – all built pyramids has been the basis for a number of theories. The reality has more to do with the fact that a pyramid is a strong and stable structure.

In truth, there are more differences than similarities between the pyramids of the Americas and those of Egypt. Most notably, Egyptian pyramids are not intended to be used; they were tombs and monuments designed to impress the observer with the greatness of the occupant. South American pyramids, on the other hand, were working buildings – they sometimes contained tombs but they were primarily temples.

Whereas Egyptian pyramids were of dressed stone and intended to stand forever, South American pyramids often used small stones retained by walls of heavier blocks in their construction, and were rebuilt whether they needed it or not. This suggests that the apparent correlation between pyramid building in different parts of the world is simply down to the constraints of the materials and techniques available.

in which shamans took on aspects of other creatures. The masks and mind-altering drugs may have played an important part in these rituals.

The Nazca civilization began to decline around 500 AD, probably as a result of climatic changes. There is evidence of widespread flooding and also severe erosion caused by deforestation to make room for crops. By 750 AD, the Nazca culture had collapsed entirely.

## THE MIDDLE HORIZON

The period 600–1000 AD is generally associated with the Middle Horizon in South America, characterized by stable and advanced cultures. Like all attempts to label eras or periods, the boundaries of the Middle Horizon are fuzzy, with some of its characteristic cultures existing outside of the neatly defined time frame.

The Sican culture is thought to have been founded around 750 AD by members of the declining Moche culture, who moved north into the Lambayeque Valley. The Sican (or Lambayeque) culture produced characteristic pottery with a black finish, in a style first used by the Moche people. Their art and pottery evolved over time, and coppersmithing was introduced.

The Sican people were traders, who brought in goods from the northern coast of South America and from Chile to the south. They were thus exposed to ideas from other societies and consequently their civilization evolved. Among the changes that occurred were funerary practices. The manner of burial indicates that there were strong social divisions in Sican society. The poor were interred in small pits under the floor of dwellings or workplaces, while the wealthier classes received greater ostentation including large quantities of grave goods and possibly human sacrifices. In the early stages of the Sican culture, the Moche practice of burying the dead in a recumbent position was followed, but by the Middle Sican era (900–1100 AD) it had become common to bury the dead in a seated position.

Like other cultures of the region, the Sican people traded with others over considerable distances. Likewise, they built irrigation canals and grand buildings in the form of pyramids, which were used for ceremonial purposes and for burials. Construction techniques appear to have been inherited from the Moche people.

The Sican culture began to decline around 1000 AD, largely as a result of a long drought that not only reduced the food supply but also undermined confidence in the leadership and religious classes of society. The capital was moved to Túcume, ushering in the Late Sican era that ended in 1375 when the region was conquered by the Chimú culture.

BELOW: The art of the Sican culture was heavily influenced by the preceding Moche culture, though it evolved over time into a more distinctively Sican style. This was in part due to external influences encountered by Sican traders.

The Tiwanaku culture is known to have built great structures close to Lake Titicaca around 700 AD, though the culture predates these constructions by several hundred years. The site has been inhabited for much longer than that, although claims that it dates back 14,000 years or more are considered questionable. It does appear that the people of Tiwanaku in the Middle Horizon were adept in the fields of astronomy and mathematics. Tiwanaku was conquered by the Incas around 1200 AD, bringing its culture to an abrupt end.

The Wari culture, also known as Huari for its capital, was warlike. The Wari people built an empire based upon a strong agricultural base, with an extensive road network to facilitate communications and troop movements. In this, as well as artistic styles, they were influential upon the later Incas.

The Wari people traded over a wide area and produced textiles featuring complex designs. These evolved over time, from clear geometric forms to abstract designs whose meaning is difficult to discern. Likewise, their pottery displayed similar designs.

The city of Huari was built in stages as the population grew, generally in a haphazard manner. The earliest structures date from around 250 AD, with construction going on until the city was abandoned around 800 AD. Other sites were abandoned over the next two centuries, sometimes being deliberately destroyed in an apparently ritual manner. It is not clear what caused the decline of the Wari empire, but by 1000 AD the region had collapsed into small polities with no overarching authority.

BELOW: Carved from a single stone block, the Gateway of the Sun is the entrance to the Kalasasaya sacred precinct at Tiwanaku. It has depictions of winged figures of an unknown nature and a relief of the staff god, whose name is not known.

# EARLY SOUTH AMERICAN RELIGIONS

LITTLE IS KNOWN FOR sure about the religions of ancient South America. With no written records or surviving traditions, what we know is postulated from carvings, statues and depictions in gold. Various gods have been identified, but we do not know their names. Thus, early South American gods are referred to descriptively by labels such as 'the staff god'.

Numerous depictions have been found of creatures that seem part human and part animal, though whether these creatures are mid-transformation from one form to another or had this appearance permanently is open to debate. It is likely that the religion of the South American complex cultures was shamanistic in nature, and there is evidence that some cultures used psychotropic drugs to achieve an altered state of consciousness that gave access to or communication with other worlds.

The half-human creatures depicted in early temples might represent an internal transformation caused by shamanistic

The Incas had too much gold for it to be useful as currency, so instead created intricate art pieces to give glory to their gods. This depicts the sun god, Inti.

ritual, or a belief that priests really did take on the form of animals. Alternatively, the creatures might be beings encountered in the other worlds. It is possible that there is no single answer to this question; there were several major cultures and many smaller ones, each with their own beliefs.

ABOVE: The pottery of the Chiribaya culture was similar in general shape to that of other societies, but was decorated in a distinctive style that may have been a melding of many different influences.

## THE LATE INTERMEDIATE PERIOD

The Late Intermediate Period, from 1000 AD to the late 1400s, was characterized by numerous small polities. Among them was the Chiribaya culture, which had existed for centuries but reached its peak after 1000 AD. Like many cultures in the region, the Chiribaya people dwelled in river valleys in what was otherwise an inhospitably dry land.

The Chiribaya people were of mixed ancestry. Some were descended from earlier cultures and had moved into the region after their collapse, while others were descended from an earlier indigenous population. Like several other cultures in the area, theirs fell victim to extensive flooding, probably caused by warming of the Pacific waters in a phenomenon known as El Niño. The floods destroyed the irrigation system needed to support the Chiribaya population.

The former Chiribaya homelands eventually came under the domination of the Inca, but before that they were controlled by the Lupaca people, whose lands lay close to Lake Titicaca. Like many dwellers at high altitude, the Lupaca culture depended on people living in lower-lying areas to provide them with food. Their society was still extant when Spanish explorers and conquistadors arrived in the region. Its downfall was largely due to disease outbreaks resulting from contact with Europeans.

The Chimú culture arose in the 12th century AD, and grew to control areas previously the territory of the Moche and Sican cultures, among others. In doing so, the Chimú people absorbed some of the cultural identity of these former societies, adding to their artistic and religious traditions. Their success owed much to a solid agricultural base, although large amounts of revenue were also raised by demanding tribute.

The capture of the Chimú ruler by the Inca in 1470 AD brought their empire under the control of the Inca, who in turn incorporated elements of Chimú culture into their own. By this process of assimilation from one culture to the next, the Inca inherited many of the artistic traditions of earlier societies as well as their skills at building irrigation systems and monuments.

The Tairona culture of northern Colombia was extraordinarily long-lived, and successfully resisted Spanish incursions for several decades. Early Tairona structures have been dated to 200 AD, at which time the culture already had the ability to construct canals and stone buildings. Terrace farming was particularly important in the difficult terrain of Andean South America; having mastered it, the Tairona people had a strong base for their society.

The Tairona people built impressive cities supported by terrace farming, ruled by shamanistic priests. Transformation was an important part of their religion, with shamans believed to be able to communicate with supernatural realms. This is reflected in Tairona art, which includes many depictions of shamans mid-transformation as half-human, half-animal creatures. Their way of life continued even after the Spanish gained control of the region, until a large-scale revolt was put down with the destruction of cities and relocation of populations. With this, a civilization that had existed since the Early Intermediate period came to an end.

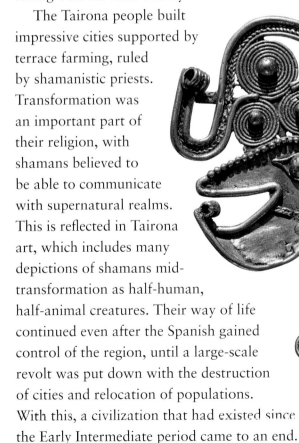

BELOW: The Tairona culture used gold and copper to make jewellery and decorative objects, and created an alloy of gold and copper that the Spanish named Tumbaga. Its composition and proportion of elements could vary widely.

CHAPTER 2

# Mesoamerican Civilizations

The move towards civilization began early in Mesoamerica, perhaps due to abundant food resources. The Maya empire was the greatest and longest-lasting of the Mesoamerican cultures, but it was influenced by other, smaller civilizations.

THE CENTRAL AMERICAN Isthmus has been joined to both northern and southern continents for around three million years. It contains varying terrain, with mountain ranges including active volcanoes and tropical lowlands. Lying as it does between two oceans, Central America receives a great deal of rainfall and is in general a humid climate. Conditions are warm to hot all year round, with no winter to speak of, though temperatures are lower at high altitude. This mix of warmth and abundant water produced conditions where many species could thrive, and the varied terrain created a range of habitats. Today, Central America is a biodiversity hotspot; in ancient times, this translated to an abundance of food and conditions where human populations could establish themselves and expand rapidly.

Dates for the entry of humans to Mesoamerica are contentious. A case has been made for evidence of habitation

OPPOSITE: Prosaically designated 'System IV' by archaeologists, this pyramid complex is among the earliest buildings constructed by the Zapotecs at Monte Alban, which grew to be among the largest cities in Mesoamerica.

dating back 20,000 or even 30,000 years, around the time of the
Last Glacial Maximum. These claims are not widely accepted,
however. It is more commonly believed that humans migrated
southwards after crossing into the Americas by the Beringia land
bridge and moved into the Americas as the ice retreated.

It is possible that the settlement of Mesoamerica took place
as a form of back-migration, with communities being set up
further south by groups moving along the coasts. People then
wandered northwards, some entering the Central American
Isthmus and others going east around the northern coast of South
America. Whether or not that is the case, it is likely that there
were some humans living in Mesoamerica by 12–10,000 BC, with
numbers increasing over time through migration and population
expansion. These early inhabitants were Neolithic hunter-
gatherers; there is evidence of mammoth hunting as well as the
taking of smaller game.

RIGHT: Artefacts such
as these Neolithic era
statuettes indicate that
humans have been living
in Mesoamerica for
10,000 years or more. The
availability of abundant
food allowed rapid
population growth, which
was necessary for the
beginnings of civilization.

Much of Mesoamerica was grassland at this time, but as the climate warmed, forests began to cover the lowlands. This forced a change in lifestyle upon the human inhabitants; by 5000 BC or so, deliberate cultivation of food crops had begun. Maize became a dietary staple, along with beans and squash. Cotton cultivation also began around the same time.

The reliable availability of food contributed to a population expansion and a move towards a sedentary lifestyle. Pottery was introduced to the region around 2300 BC, probably as a result of contact with developing cultures to the south. Another hallmark of civilization, the development of centralized authority, began as a consequence of agricultural food production. Power began to be concentrated in the hands of those who owned the best farmland, creating a ruling class. With these factors in place, the groundwork was laid for the rise of complex societies.

ABOVE: The Mayan city of Kaminaljuyu, most likely founded before 1500 BC, became a centre for ceramics production. The creation of decorative as well as functional pottery suggests that the Mayans were highly prosperous by the time this figure was made.

## ORNAMENTATION, TOOLS AND WEAPONS

In the Western world, the use of metal for tools began around 7500 BC, and was widespread by 6500 BC. This ushered in a fairly short era known as the Chalcolithic ('Copper Age') between the Neolithic (late Stone Age) and the Bronze Age. Copper had disadvantages as a material for tools, mainly its relative softness, which meant blades would lose their edge and levers would bend. However, the same factors meant that copper could be worked without extreme heating. Copper was thus the starting point for metalworking in the Western world.

Gold was similarly easy to work and, like copper, was often found in its native state. Although it might be alloyed with silver or other metals, native gold did not require a chemical process or heating to obtain its metallic form, making it another candidate for early metallurgy. Gold was far too soft for toolmaking but

RIGHT: Finds of distinctive ceramics are one of the factors that allow archaeologists to identify a site in terms of date and culture. This ceramic figure of a seated figure with a vessel dates from around 200 BC–300 AD.

could be worked into jewellery, figurines or other ornamentation. It is not clear exactly when coppersmithing began in Mesoamerica, but there is evidence of smelting from around 200 BC; gold items began to appear 400–500 years later. Whereas metalworking was apparently essential to the development of Western civilization, the early civilizations of Mesoamerica created their cities and built their empires entirely without metal tools, and even the later cultures made relatively little practical use of metal.

Many alternative materials were available, notably stone, wood and bone, all of which had been in use for millennia. Techniques for creating tools and weapons out of these materials were highly advanced; in many cases, an item made from these 'primitive' materials was as effective as one made from bronze or even iron. A bone-tipped arrow was just as lethal as an iron-tipped one under most circumstances, and a stone-headed mace hit as hard as a metal one.

The lack of metal made some weapons – notably cutting implements – difficult to produce. A stone-headed axe could be very effective and a wooden sword could carry a surprisingly sharp edge, but the creation of a blade capable of cutting deeply or precisely was a problem without metal. The solution, for Mesoamerican societies, was to use obsidian.

BELOW: Lacking the ability to craft blades from metal, the Maya produced equally lethal implements by flaking obsidian to create an incredibly sharp edge. This dagger was used for bloodletting and human sacrifice.

Obsidian is naturally occurring volcanic glass, which is created where lava cools very quickly such as on contact with water. It is usually black but can be dark brown or green, and was readily available in some parts of Mesoamerica. Obsidian could be easily flaked to create an extremely sharp – if not very durable – edge using techniques similar to those that produced flint tools in Neolithic times.

Common obsidian tools included small handheld blades used to cut or scrape, while larger implements could be constructed by fashioning a handle or main component out of wood and adding microliths – small pieces of flaked obsidian – to the edges. If done precisely, this could create a composite weapon or tool that rivalled any metal implement in sharpness and that could be repaired if the edge were damaged. Obsidian could also be polished to a mirror finish, and was used for decoration as well as practical purposes.

Obsidian never really became obsolete. It remained useful even after metallurgy finally reached Mesoamerica and indeed still has some uses today. Its plentiful availability was one reason for the late development of metalworking. There was simply no need to go through the long process of mastering a new technique when something as good was already available.

Without the need for blades and with other tools already available, early metalworking tended towards decorative items. Copper and gold were initially worked without melting, although later Mesoamerican metalsmiths became adept at smelting metal ore and creating alloys. These were largely aimed at giving the end product a pleasing colour rather

BELOW: Axe-shaped copper artefacts are found at many sites, especially in tombs. Sometimes referred to as axe-monies, these items are thought to have been used as currency in some areas.

than great strength, and this required very precise technique in addition to a detailed knowledge of the effects of different composition on the final colour.

Large-scale manufacture of copper tools seems to have begun around 600 AD, with bronze appearing later. There was, however, no real 'copper age' or 'bronze age' in Mesoamerica; elsewhere, these technologies defined the limits of what could be achieved and characterized eras of history. In Mesoamerica, metal tools were an alternative to those that already existed, and society had already progressed past the stage reached by Bronze or Copper Age cultures elsewhere.

Although the late adoption of widespread use of metal items did not hold back the cultural development of the Mesoamerican civilizations, it did preclude the development of some technologies. Although not a 'dead end' as such, the reliance on natural materials such as wood and obsidian did slow down progress in some areas. If the Mesoamericans had adopted bronze-working and later ironsmithing on a similar timeframe to Europeans – which they certainly had the capability to do – then the arrival of Europeans in the Americas might have gone very differently.

## LANGUAGE IN MESOAMERICA

The first people into the Americas were behaviourally modern humans. That is, since around 40–50,000 years ago, during the Last Glacial Maximum, humans underwent a rapid change in behaviour that set them apart from smart, tool-using animals. These traits expressed themselves in the form of abstract thought, language, forward planning and artistic means such as art and music.

Language crystallizes thought for the speaker and conveys his or her ideas to others. Some of the ideas put forward by the early modern humans were undoubtedly as inane or silly as any modern conversation. Others were profound questions about the nature of being or what might be over the next hill. Experiences were shared and knowledge passed on, enabling a group to establish a base of knowledge beyond the personal experiences of each member.

OPPOSITE: The Mayan site at Copán in Honduras contains many stelae carved with complex glyphs that can represent a single word or a syllable. Glyphs are read in pairs from the top, moving down to the next pair.

The nature of what is said, and what needs to be said, guides the formation of a language just as what is said influences the thinking of others and the behaviour of the group. Thus, as humans spread through Mesoamerica, their different experiences and differing communication needs resulted in the development of language families that diverged from one another. Within each family, languages were related – initially closely – but diverged over time to become more distinct. A speaker of one member language might note only occasional differences when talking to someone whose native tongue was a close member of the same family, but might be able to piece together what they were saying only with great difficulty if their languages had diverged due to time or geographical separation.

The Proto-Mayan language is thought to have appeared around 3000 BC or earlier, and diverged into subgroups over time. There is little direct evidence of its form or even existence, but the Mayan language family must have developed from a common root. Over time, this root language developed in different ways among various groups of speakers, creating a large number of Mayan tongues the descendants of which are still spoken today.

The Oto-Manguean language family appeared around 2000 BC and diverged into two main groups as a result of geographical influences. These were further subdivided, creating an extremely varied language

BELOW: After contact with the Spanish, the Maya recorded their beliefs in an attempt to preserve them. The Florentine Codex is one of the few of their books to have escaped destruction at the hands of zealous missionaries.

group. Among the Oto-Manguean languages was the tongue spoken by the Zapotec civilization. The third major language family included proto-Mixean and proto-Zoquean as its main branches, and is named Mixe-Zoque for them. It is thought that the Olmec people spoke a language from this family.

The Uto-Aztecan language family originated outside Mesoamerica and includes languages spoken by the tribes of North America as well as the Aztecs and their related cultures. It was by way of the Aztecs that the first Europeans into the Americas learned of the earlier civilizations in Mesoamerica, with the result that many names and concepts are based on what the Aztecs called them rather than the original names used by the people of that place and time.

> The earliest known civilization in Mesoamerica developed in the lowlands of what is now Mexico, this was a gradual process.

Thus, in some cases our understanding of ancient concepts must be questioned. It has been filtered through the interpretation of the Aztecs who may not have fully understood the earlier cultures of the region, then translated into Spanish by people with a very different way of thinking and some cast-iron preconceptions about the nature of the Americas and their people. It is reasonable to expect that, five hundred years later, some of the original meaning may have been lost in translation.

## THE OLMEC CIVILIZATION

The earliest known civilization in Mesoamerica developed in the lowlands of what is now Mexico. This was a gradual process, following on from earlier cultures in the surrounding region. From them the Olmecs inherited many cultural traits as well as technological capabilities, and in time later civilizations would adopt the same customs.

The Olmecs, as we call them, left behind no written records. What is known about them comes from archaeological evidence or secondary sources such as other, later cultures. Even the name we give them comes from outside their culture. It is an Aztec word meaning 'rubber people', referring to their use of rubber

RIGHT: The site at La
Venta contains four of
the colossal stone heads
associated with the Olmec
civilization as well as
numerous altars carved in
the distinctive Olmec style,
which influenced later
Mesoamerican cultures.

for a number of purposes, including the creating of balls for the
ceremonial ball game.

Exactly when the Olmec civilization became recognizable as
such is open to some debate, but it appears that its hallmarks –
notably the distinctive style of art – were present around 1500 BC.
This makes the early Olmecs contemporary with ancient Egypt,
Babylonia and the earliest known civilization in China.

The social elite in Olmec society were landowners, priests and
skilled craftspeople. There does not appear to have been a military
class as such, although Olmec society did contain warriors. The
upper echelons of society were concentrated in small cities, with
most of the population dispersed among farmlands. Trade was
facilitated by the river valleys of the region, allowing luxury
goods to be brought to the cities, and the society was sufficiently
prosperous to permit the accrual of such status symbols.

Among the luxury goods enjoyed by the Olmec elite were
items carved of jade. Jade carving began before 1500 BC, and
was a well-advanced art during the Olmec era. Indeed, jade face

masks in a distinctive style were one of the hallmarks used to designate an archaeological site as being Olmec as opposed to one of the later Mesoamerican civilizations.

Carvings in jade and similar materials took many forms, though often with common features. Face masks and votive axes both commonly feature a cleft in the forehead and attributes of both humans and animals. These carvings were apparently traded beyond the Olmec homeland; carved artefacts of Olmec origin have been found at Maya sites.

## SAN LORENZO

The oldest known Olmec site is San Lorenzo, which had a recognizably Olmec character by 1200 BC. The settlement was built on a natural plateau that was modified with earthworks to make it more suitable for construction. San Lorenzo was destroyed around 900 BC; its large carved stone monuments were defaced, toppled and buried. This represented a lot of effort, although it is not clear who went to such trouble to wreck the San Lorenzo site. The Olmec civilization continued to develop after the fall of San Lorenzo, which may have been part of an internal power struggle or a takeover by some outside power. The Olmec site at La Venta replaced San Lorenzo and between 800–400 BC was the centre of the Olmec civilization. However, Olmec society went into a decline and after 400 BC it had been supplanted by other cultures.

The Olmec civilization was extremely influential on the development of other Mesoamerican cultures, in terms of religion, art, social organization and technology. Metal tools were not in use, but curved mirrors of polished iron have been found in Olmec sites. Their art objects were clearly prized by other cultures; they were traded while the Olmec civilization was in its heyday and may have been plundered afterwards. Olmec artefacts are found in archaeological sites from cultures that existed much later, suggesting that they were valued as relics of former times or perhaps just beautiful objects in their own right.

BELOW: Explorer Baron Alexander von Humboldt was given this Olmec axe during his expedition to South and Central America. The lack of knowledge about the region meant that it was misidentified as Aztec.

# THE OLMEC CALENDAR

THE OLMECS INVENTED a dating system based on the solar cycle. It contained 18 months of 20 days, plus five additional days to make 365. These days were considered to be unlucky by the Maya, who used the Olmec system (as did many other Mesoamerican cultures), although it is not clear if the concept of 'unlucky days' originated with the Olmecs themselves. The Olmec calendar did not contain leap years or any other way of compensating for the quarter-day discrepancy between the solar year and the 365-day year.

The Olmec calendar was later combined with the 260-day sacred round to create what is now known as the Mesoamerican calendar. Combining the two gives a unique name for each day in a 52-year cycle. It is not clear why the 260-day cycle was created, though it could be simply the significance of the numbers 13 and 20 in Mesoamerican mythology and society. There is considerable evidence that the sacred cycle was tied to the planting season by way of observation of the constellations.

Although the Olmecs did not invent the whole Mesoamerican calendar, they laid the groundwork for it and established the habit of using the solar cycle. This persisted after their civilization had evolved, by way of the Epi-Olmec culture, into something that was no longer Olmec in nature.

It is not clear what caused the decline of the first great civilization of Mesoamerica. Conflict is always a possibility, as is changing climate conditions. Disaster has also been postulated; the Olmec lived in a region with active volcanoes that may have produced large quantities of ash. This could be sufficient to clog irrigation systems and make food-producing areas untenable even if the destruction was small. The local terrain meant that Olmec food production was intensive and restricted to fairly small areas. Even a modest eruption in the right place could cause a famine.

It is possible that the Olmec civilization fell victim to a number of smaller problems that gradually became too much to deal with. Tensions within an evolving society, combined with reduced food production, could have sent the Olmec civilization into a downward spiral from which it could not recover.

The Olmec civilization was not destroyed, conquered or otherwise obliterated. Instead its cultural cohesion dissipated and what remained of it evolved into a form that was no longer recognizably Olmec. The third major centre of Olmec society, Tres Zapotes, remained as a remnant or Epi-Olmec (post-Olmec) society and was for many years an important centre in Mesoamerican civilization. Tres Zapotes was never as grand as the earlier centres and produced art that gradually lost its characteristic Olmec features in favour of influences from elsewhere.

BELOW: Probably created between 1502–1521, the Aztec 'Sun Stone' incorporates a calendar based on the much earlier Olmec solar cycle. It is normally displayed in a vertical position but would originally have lain flat.

## OLMEC RELIGION

Little is known for sure about the Olmec religion, other than that they revered elements of the natural world. We do not know the names of their gods, so they are referred to by numbers or descriptions of their images by modern historians. These gods represented natural phenomena such as rain and important resources such as maize.

Olmec religion is also associated with powerful animals such as eagles, sharks and, most of all, jaguars. It is possible that the cleft forehead depicted on many face masks and carvings represented the forehead of a jaguar. Other jaguar features are also present in carvings, giving rise to the theory that the Olmec culture worshipped a 'were-jaguar' as one of their gods. The hypothesis that this were-jaguar was the supreme Olmec deity was accepted for some time but has been challenged.

Depictions of other human-animal creatures suggest that the were-jaguar was one of many gods, and by no means necessarily superior to any of them. However, the image of the Olmec as 'children of the were-jaguar' has become popularized and is unlikely to be dispelled in the near future.

## OLMEC ART

The Olmec civilization produced cave paintings and small art objects such as carvings in wood or greenstone, but its most famous creations are large

BELOW: Jaguars feature prominently in Olmec art, often (as here) associated with priests. Depictions often feature a part-human, part-animal 'were-jaguar' creature which has come to represent the Olmecs in the popular imagination.

# AUTOSACRIFICE IN OLMEC RELIGION

MANY CULTURES CONSIDERED BLOOD to have spiritual power and used it in their rituals. For the Olmecs, blood was symbolic of fertility and was used in rituals intended to ensure good harvests as well as more generally in acts of worship. The act of bloodletting was part of the ceremony, permitting contact with the supernatural world, and was carried out by the subject on their own body. Bloodletting implements might be carved form jade or bone, although shark teeth and the spines of stingrays were also used.

Bloodletting could be on quite a small scale, with a drop or two drawn from the finger or thumb with a cactus needle or specialized instrument. Greater sacrifices were made by piercing the tongue, genitals or other soft parts of the body. Observers of later Mesoamerican cultures that inherited some practices from the Olmecs wrote of mass ceremonies in which cords were drawn through the pierced parts of several participants, linking them in a common bloodletting. This practice may have originated with the Olmecs.

RIGHT: A jade perforator used in Autosacrifice or bloodletting.

stone sculptures. These include what appear to be highly ornamented thrones that may have been used for ceremonial occasions, and colossal stone heads.

The heads are highly realistic, and appear to depict rulers or players in the ceremonial ball game. Each has a different headdress, although the significance of this is unclear. Most of the heads were carved from boulders, although two have been found that were originally part of a stone throne.

The smallest of the heads weighs six tons, while the largest are in the 40–50 ton range. The heads were moved from the source of the stone to their points of display by an unknown means. The Olmecs did not use wheeled vehicles and no suitable beasts of burden were available to assist, so this undertaking must have been carried out entirely by teams of workers. The level of organization required to move such large objects is impressive,

ABOVE: The discovery of Olmec colossal stone heads with apparently 'African' features sparked much speculation about contact with other continents. There is no evidence of this occurring, however.

suggesting that the Olmecs possessed highly centralized authority at the time the stones were carved. Most date from the Early Pre-Classic era of the Olmec civilization, between 1500 and 1000 BC. Other cultures in the Americas were capable of undertaking great works at this time or even earlier, but the construction of a building typically involved moving and placing smaller individual elements than the stone heads of the Olmecs.

Olmec cave paintings depict jaguar-headed people similar to those found in carvings, and in many cases feature aspects of Olmec society that otherwise could only be guessed at.

Rulers, priests or members of the elite class are depicted sitting on huge carved thrones similar to those found in the Olmec heartland, suggesting that the thrones were functional rather than representational.

## CEREMONIAL BALL GAME

The ceremonial ball game was played by several Mesoamerican cultures, of which the Olmec civilization is the oldest. The Olmecs may have invented the game or might have inherited a version of it from earlier people. The Olmecs were the earliest society to build the distinctive I-shaped ball court used for the game, so can be credited with developing the game into its distinctive form even if they were not its inventors. Various forms of ball game have existed over time, but in the definitive version, players are permitted only to use their hips to move the ball.

The earliest evidence of the ball game dates from around 1700 BC, and takes the form of carved figurines depicting players. Rubber balls used in the game have been found, with the earliest dating from around 1600 BC, while the oldest known ball court was constructed around 1400 BC. This coincides with the early phase of the Olmec civilization, at which time strong central authority is known to have existed. Ball courts were built close to the dwellings of leaders; the ability to host games was a symbol of status and wealth.

The ball game was more than a sporting contest. In addition to the social aspects, religious ceremonies were carried out at the beginning and end of the game, and indeed the whole contest might be considered a ritual. There are no accounts of how the Olmecs played the ball game, but it was incorporated into the religions of the Aztec

BELOW: It is thought that Hachas in the form of a human head (below) may have replaced actual severed heads used to mark the court during a ceremonial ball game, or presented as trophies.

# ERAS IN MESOAMERICAN HISTORY

THE PREHISTORY AND HISTORY of Mesoamerica is generalized into distinct eras, characterized by technology and cultural behaviour. The Paleo-Indian, or Lithic, period begins with the earliest habitation of the region, until around 7–8000 BC. This was followed by the Archaic period, which came to a gradual end from 3500 to 2000 BC. By this time, key technologies such as pottery were becoming available, enabling social development and the rise of centralized cultures.

Running from the end of the Archaic era to around 250 AD, the Pre-Classic or Formative era saw the beginnings of the quintessential Mesoamerican culture elements. Pyramids and large-scale irrigation systems were undertaken, and the Mesoamerican calendar appeared, possibly in connection with major agricultural expansion. The practice of human sacrifice was well established by the end of the Pre-Classic era. Pre-Classic civilizations include the Olmec and Epi-Olmec, Teotihuacán and early Maya cultures.

The Classic period of Mesoamerican history runs from 250 AD to 900 AD. The Maya Empire was at its height, while the Olmec civilization declined in the latter part of the era and Teotihuacán was destroyed at the end of the Classic era. Numerous small semi-independent states also existed within a shifting web of alliances, often coming under the influence of the greater powers. The Post-Classic era, after 900 AD until the arrival of Europeans in Mesoamerica, saw a mix of cultural decline and technological advancement.

The Toltec civilization arose after 900 AD and the Maya – although diminished – survived to meet the European incursions. The Maya succumbed to Spanish conquest during the 1500s and 1600s along with the recently arisen Aztec empire. The period from 1521 onwards is known as the Colonial era, lasting almost into modern times.

LEFT: In the Americas the population went on using stone and obsidian for ever more sophisticated building purposes.

and Maya civilizations. Maya legends depict the ball game as a clash between humans and beings from the underworld, while the Aztecs are known to have sacrificed the losing team on some occasions.

### THE ZAPOTEC CIVILIZATION

Centred in the Oaxaca valley region of what is now Mexico, the Zapotec civilization initially had its capital at Monte Albán. There is evidence

The Maya gradually succumbed to Spanish conquest during the 1500s and 1600s along with the recently arisen Aztec Empire.

of considerable conflict in the area in the years before the appearance of the Monte Albán site, with several communities destroyed, which suggests that it was founded as the capital of an emerging state created by conquest or victory in an ongoing power struggle.

Monte Albán stood on high ground, levelled off and terraced. The earliest structures on the site date from 800 BC or earlier, although these were built over by later construction. The city's central area contained large plazas and a ceremonial ball court as well as pyramids, and was surrounded by a large residential district. The city could accommodate more than 15,000 people in its heyday, and was the capital of the Zapotec civilization until its eclipse by Mitla.

The Monte Albán site poses a number of questions for historians. Its location was clearly a deliberate choice; it replaced the city of San José Mogote as the capital of the local region and was apparently founded for that purpose. However, while its location was certainly defensible, it lacked a water source and was sufficiently distant from the nearest food production so that supplying the population would be a problem. The presence of structures that could have been used for astronomical purposes suggests that religion played a part in the choice of location, although it is equally possible that the driving factor was visibility – the monumental structures of the city could be seen from much of the surrounding valley. The power of Monte Albán grew from around 500 BC to 150 BC, during which time the Oaxaca valley region was brought under central control. The city saw extensive redevelopment during the next century, serving as capital to the Zapotec until it began to decline for reasons that remain unclear. By 900 AD it was abandoned and the capital had moved to Mitla. The Zapotec civilization was highly organized and capable of undertaking large-scale engineering works such as terracing the hillsides around Monte Albán and setting up an irrigation system. Just getting the stone to build the new city into place was a difficult undertaking, and feeding the population of the city required a sophisticated logistics system.

The Zapotec people were adept traders, forming links with the Olmec civilization early in their history and later trading with the Maya and Teotihuacán cultures. Relations with the latter appear to have been close; the city of Teotihuacán hosted a permanent

BELOW: Standing around 400m (1312ft) above the Valley of Oaxaca, Monte Albán was occupied for around 1400 years, and even after its abandonment the site seems to have retained some significance for the local population.

or semi-permanent Zapotec population. Not surprisingly, the Zapotec people shared many cultural traits with other Mesoamerican cultures, including the ceremonial ball game and a similar style of art.

Zapotec religion was complex, with deities representing important concepts such as war and fertility or natural phenomena such as rain. Gods were depicted with human and animal or supernatural features. In addition to the major gods of the pantheon, there were local deities associated with particular cities; ancestors were also venerated. Temple reliefs indicate that the Zapotec people practised the ritual sacrifice of prisoners taken in war. Zapotec reliefs also indicate the existence of an alphabet.

The earliest known writings in the Americas are carved on the temple of the Danzantes at Monte Albán. The temple is the

oldest surviving structure in the city, and dates from its founding. Like many such structures, the temple's original name is lost to history, and its modern title is a misnomer. The carvings on its walls, depicting people twisted into unnatural shapes, were originally thought to be of dancers. It is now generally accepted that they are mutilated human sacrifices.

The Zapotec civilization declined after 900 AD, for reasons that are unclear. Conflict was common at this time, and although there was no violent destruction of Zapotec society, it may be that trade or food production – or both – were sufficiently disrupted to cause a terminal decline. After the capital was moved to Mitla, the Zapotec culture continued in diminished form for many years. Mitla was still occupied when the Spanish arrived in the Americas.

The remnant of the Zapotec civilization at first attempted to avoid conflict with the newcomers. The Zapotec had been in conflict with the Aztec empire, so may have hoped that the conqueror of their enemy might be a friend – or at least

BELOW: After the decline of Monte Albán, the Zapotec capital moved to Mitla. Like Monte Albán, the site has been given a modern name, but in this case the Nahuatl word Mitla is fairly close to the Zapotec 'Lyobaa' which means 'place of rest' or 'tomb'.

amenable to accepting tribute. This did not last long, however, and the Zapotec lands were conquered – if not entirely pacified – in the 1520s.

## THE TEOTIHUACÁN CIVILIZATION

As with other civilizations of pre-Columbian Mesoamerica, modern scholars do not know what the people of what we name the Teotihuacan civilization called themselves. Carvings have been located that may include a self-name, but it has not been possible to translate them. Thus, this culture has become known by the Aztec word for their capital, which means 'place of the gods'.

Teotihuacán may have been the capital of a large organized state. It is possible that there was some form of Teotihuacán empire at least for a time, but more probably Teotihuacán was a city-state that exerted huge cultural and political influence but did not directly rule other cities. Teotihuacán was an important trade centre, with textiles and other trade goods manufactured in the city. Significant populations from other cultures dwelled in Teotihuacán, conducting both trade and cultural exchange with the local population.

Teotihuacán was founded around 100 BC, although the site may have been inhabited before that. It reached its greatest extent in the 4th century AD, with a population possibly as high as 200,000. Feeding all these people required sophisticated

ABOVE: Like most polytheistic cultures the Zapotecs worshipped gods associated with agriculture and plenty. The importance of maize is obvious from the god's headdress, which also features the face of the rain and storm god Cocijo.

ABOVE: **Many stone masks were found at Teotihuacán and were long assumed to have been produced there. There is now evidence that at least some of the masks were carved far from Teotihuacán, perhaps at Puebla.**

irrigation and agricultural network combined with effective storage, inventory and distribution of food. Agriculture used the chinampa system, which was later adopted by the Aztec empire. Artificial islands were constructed in deliberately flooded areas, using layers of earth and vegetation atop rafts. Several of these islands, some 100–200m (328–656ft) long and up to 20m (66ft) wide, ran side by side, creating rich growing conditions. Intensive farming methods made the large population possible and helped concentrate power among the elite. Teotihuacán may not have had an empire as such, but it had sufficient military power to deter attack and to induce compliance from smaller city-states. These may have been tributary states, either outright or as part of a trade agreement that favoured Teotihuacán. Those who acted against the interests of their powerful neighbour risked attack by Teotihuacán's warriors.

Warriors are depicted wearing shell goggles and headdresses, which may have been intended to denote status or to inspire fear in the enemy, and with a 'mirror' on their backs. This was a stone disc with an inlay of pieces of iron pyrites, possibly also adorned with feathers. They were protected by rectangular shields and armed with javelins or darts thrown with the assistance of an atlatl.

'Atlatl' is an Aztec word that is applied to spear-throwers of this sort, but the device was invented long before the Aztecs or even the people of Teotihuacán trod the Earth. It dates from the late Stone Age or even earlier, and can be fashioned with very basic tools. Rather than hold the spear or dart fully in his hand, the hunter or warrior gripped the shaft of the atlatl with three fingers and placed his thumb along its back. The short throwing

# CHINAMPAS IN THE AMERICAS

THE CHINAMPA, OR 'RAISED FIELD', system was used in Mesoamerica and among the Andean civilizations. A lake or area of wetlands could be converted to agricultural land in this manner, even if the surrounding terrain was not suitable for farming. This was the case in the highlands of Bolivia and Peru, where a raised field system permitted agriculture in the Lake Titicaca area that was otherwise unproductive.

The process of creating a raised field system was laborious, requiring the digging of drainage ditches, the building of causeways and dykes, and the creation of rafts to support the artificial islands where food would be grown. Water levels had to be evened out and controlled, after which the farming islands could be established. These were built up with soil and vegetable matter that had to be brought to the site along with construction materials.

Once all these tasks were completed then farming could begin. In addition to the usual work of caring for the crops, the water system had to be monitored and maintained. This did allow some otherwise destructive events such as flooding to be controlled, but it was a complex and continuous endeavour. A period of neglect could wreck the whole system with catastrophic effects.

The chinampa system has been erroneously described as using fields floating on rafts in a lake. In fact a raft-like structure may be used as a base, but the mass of soil and plants forms an artificial island.

BELOW: **Warriors
and priests in many
Mesoamerican cultures
were associated with
birds. This ceramic figure
from Teotihuacán appears
to depict an important
individual in ceremonial
costume, adorned with
plumes and feathers.**

spear was supported with one finger hooked over it and by a projection at the base of the atlatl that fitted into a notch on the base of the spear.

Essentially, the user made a throwing motion with the atlatl, which in turn projected the spear with greater velocity than could otherwise be achieved. The atlatl reduced the amount of interaction between the user's hand and the spear, removing some sources of inaccuracy. The result was a weapon that flew further, hit harder and was more precise than a hand-hurled spear.

Warriors who fought with atlatl and spear used techniques similar to ancient hunters rather than soldiers. Loading a spear on to the atlatl took scarcely longer than picking one up in the hand, at least for a skilled user, but a warrior had only one shot before 'reloading' was necessary and could only carry so many spears. His shield offered effective protection against the projectiles of enemies, so a fight between two groups of warriors who relied solely on these weapons might take the form of a protracted and perhaps inconclusive skirmish.

Other weapons were used for close combat. There is evidence of maces or war clubs throughout Central and South America, both in the form of artworks and surviving mace heads. These were of stone, polished to the desired weight and dimensions, creating an effective personal weapon without the use of metal.

Spears with an obsidian head may have been used for personal combat. They occasionally appear in art, and objects resembling spearheads have been found. Wooden shafts are much less likely to survive, so their absence does not imply that they were not in use. Likewise, the main component of the obsidian-edged macuahuitl sword was made of wood, so the only likely finds indicating these weapons were in use would be obsidian shards. These could have had other uses, but depictions of figures armed with such weapons survive so it is likely that it was in use.

The decorative headdress, mirror and goggles of the Mesoamerican warrior offered little physical protection but may have had a spiritual role. The warriors of Teotihuacán, like those of some other Mesoamerican cultures, wore regalia associated with different kinds of animals. This created a group identity, fostering esprit de corps that contributed to fighting effectiveness even if it had no otherworldly significance.

Other cultures, including many Native American tribes, created armour that looks ineffective but that was believed to imbue the wearer with magical protection. It may be that the accoutrements of the Mesoamerican warrior were similar in fiction, although some aspects of military dress are also found in the daily clothing of the Teotihuacán elite. This might be nothing more than an affectation or fashion, or could indicate status in society based on previous military success. It is also possible that the same spiritual benefits gained by warriors were desired by political and economic figures too.

ABOVE: Many jade masks found throughout Mesoamerica were produced in the Teotihuacán style. A number of those in modern collections have been revealed as fakes by examination of the distinctive marks left by modern tools.

## RELIGION AND ARCHITECTURE IN TEOTIHUACÁN

Teotihuacán was clearly a carefully planned city, either from the outset or when early construction was built over. The city was laid out on a grid pattern, with a central avenue (known as the Avenue of the Dead) leading to the religious district dominated by two great pyramids. There is evidence that there were once two avenues, running at right angles, subdividing the city.

Within the grid pattern were residential areas, markets, workplaces and smaller temples. It appears that the city also had districts devoted to people from other cultures – Zapotec and Maya, for example. These were in different parts of the city and kept separate from one another.

The dominant architectural features of Teotihuacán were the great pyramids of the Sun and the Moon. The Pyramid of the Sun is one of the largest pyramids in the world. Construction began around 100 AD, apparently over other buildings, the remains of which were found during modern archaeological exploration of

the structure. Tunnels and caves have also been found under the pyramid, whose function is unknown. It is presumed that it was originally a temple, but this remains unproven.

The Pyramid of the Moon was built in stages between 200 and 450 AD. Although smaller than the Pyramid of the Sun, it is still a huge construction. It was built over an earlier, much lower, structure thought to have been connected with astronomical events and thus perhaps tied to predicting the planting or wet season. The pyramid lies at the end of the Avenue of the Dead and is thought to have been a temple dedicated to ensuring the

LEFT: The Avenue of the Dead in Teotihuacán leads to this point. During rainy-season ceremonies the blood of victims hurled down the pyramid steps would be washed along the avenue creating the impression of a life-giving river.

ABOVE: The most famous fresco at Teotihuacán depicts the 'Paradise of Tlaloc', though the role of the rain-god Tlaloc is apparently taken by a female goddess referred to as the Great Goddess of Teotihuacán.

city was adequately supplied with water. Viewed from the Avenue of the Dead, the pyramid is backed by Cerro Gordo ('fat hill') behind it, and is constructed with similar proportions.

A mural found in the palace of Tepantitla, where religious leaders of the city dwelled, depicts a mountain that may be Cerro Gordo, from which life-giving waters flow. Many of the people in the mural are able to live happy, productive lives as a result and are going about normal activities. However, the mountain is being fed a stream of human sacrifices, presumably to keep the water flowing. The mural is called the 'Paradise of Tlaloc', after a god worshipped in Mesoamerica. The 'Tlaloc' figure in this mural appears to be female, and has been dubbed the Great Goddess of Teotihuacán. She is depicted in statuary elsewhere in the city, and appears to have water flowing through or from her hands.

The third largest structure in Teotihuacán is known as the temple of the feathered serpent, after a god similar to the deity called Quetzalcóatl by the Aztecs. This may be an early representation of the same deity or a completely different god with a similar appearance. The pyramid was the site of a great many human sacrifices, but appears to have diminished in importance later in the city's history.

Teotihuacán contains numerous other temples and palaces that were probably the residence of priests. However, there is little evidence of centralized authority in the form of a king or chief priest. It appears that a large religious class provided leadership as well as religious functions. This would include law and order as well; the mountain needed regular sacrifices and the threat of becoming one might be an effective deterrent to crime. Today the plazas and structures are named for their surviving features, such as the Palace of Jaguars, which houses murals of jaguars, or the Palace of Quetzalpapalotl, named for an initial impression of butterfly-birds in its surviving art.

At its height, Teotihuacán may have been home to as many as 200,000 people. The nature of its society is evident in the construction and architecture of the city. It is highly organized, with great temples but no royal palace or similar structure. There is accommodation for a large priestly class, but few indications of an uppermost echelon that ruled the others. It may be that the society of Teotihuacán was less stratified than many other Mesoamerican cultures, with power shared among the priests and

BELOW: The Palace of the Jaguars is named for its murals with their complex imagery depicting jaguar-like creatures engaged in a variety of mysterious activities. One is apparently blowing through a conch shell whilst another sits atop a red serpent.

religious leaders and the lower echelons of society kept pacified by their religion. On the one hand, compliance and contentment meant a prosperous life; on the other, troublemaking might lead to a more fatal contribution to the city's continued well-being.

Teotihuacán reached the peak of its power around 375–500 AD. Around 600 AD, much of the city was destroyed under circumstances that remain unclear. The destruction of religious stonework and art objects suggests an internal uprising or perhaps outside conquest. If the latter was the case, the city-state of Xochicalco, at the time beginning its rise to prominence, may have been responsible.

Teotihuacán was not completely destroyed, but its power was broken. Although the city was inhabited over the next centuries, it never regained any degree of importance. Xochicalco replaced Teotihuacán as a political centre to a great extent, but it was abandoned around 900 AD, like many similar sites. Nonetheless, Teotihuacán continued to exert a major cultural influence on the Toltec and later civilizations.

# THE MACUAHUITL

THE MACUAHUITL WAS PRODUCED in many varieties, just as more conventional metal swords were. One- and two-handed versions were used, with varying designs of obsidian teeth. Some variants left quite large gaps between the teeth; others created a near-continuous cutting edge. Although extremely sharp, a cutting surface made of several obsidian blades would not slice flesh quite the same way as a continuous metal edge might. A slashing blow would be more likely to cause a wide surface injury than to cut deep into flesh. This might be to the advantage of the ambitious Mesoamerican warrior, since killing an enemy was less well regarded as wounding one and forcing him to surrender for later sacrifice.

The macuahuitl was an offensively orientated weapon, with no hand protection and a fragile cutting edge unsuited to parrying an attack. It was probably used in a highly mobile 'slash and dash' style of combat, with warriors darting in to cut at their enemies then dodging away. This required an individualistic style of combat rather than the close order that became prevalent in European pre-gunpowder conflict. Given the terrain over which the Mesoamerican warrior often fought, open order was a better tactical choice anyway.

The Aztec empire considered Teotihuacán to be the birthplace of civilization and an ancient holy site; their leaders visited the city to seek the favour of the gods. Many of the beings depicted in the carvings of Teotihuacán, such as the feathered serpent, were revered as gods by later societies. Thus, although it was not the first civilization in Mesoamerica, Teotihuacán was arguably the most influential.

ABOVE: This image from the Florentine Codex depicts Aztec warriors armed with macuahuitl, an obsidian-edged sword-club which was developed by earlier Mesoamerican civilizations. The figures appear to be elite Eagle and Jaguar warriors.

## THE TOLTEC CIVILIZATION

The Toltec civilization was founded around 900 AD, a time of considerable upheaval in Mesoamerica. It may be that the early Toltecs took advantage of the misfortunes of the Olmec, Zapotec and Teotihuacán civilizations to begin their rise to power, although what part they played in the decline of these cultures is open to debate. Most of what is known about the Toltecs is derived from Aztec legends, which are inevitably distorted.

According to Aztec traditions, the first great leader of the Toltecs was Mixcóatl, who presided over the destruction of Teotihuacán. The influence of Teotihuacán was strong, whether as a result of earlier contact or during the conquest of the city, and Mixcóatl's son, Ce Acatl Topiltzin, took the title of Quetzalcóatl after the feathered serpent god depicted in the temples of Teotihuacán.

The Toltecs built an empire in what is now central Mexico, establishing a capital at Tollan from which the name given to their culture derives. According to Aztec lore, this was a marvellous place, with abundant crops and learned people capable of undertaking great works more or less at whim. The people of Tollan had the favour of the gods and did not need to do much to appease them. This was largely due to the religious leadership of Ce Acatl Topiltzin, who lived to a great age before finally being undone by his enemy, the god Tezcatlipoca.

The earliest known consumption of chocolate was around 1900 BC, when the Olmecs introduced a drink made from the cacao bean.

Tezcatlipoca tricked the ancient priest into abandoning his sacred duties, causing misfortune to fall upon the Toltecs. Ce Acatl Topiltzin left Tollan and wandered for a time, while his home city was destroyed. The fate of Ce Acatl Topiltzin varies from one tale to another. In some he sailed away out to sea on a raft of serpents; in others he became the morning star after self-immolating as atonement for his errors. Maya legends contain a similar story about a great leader they called Kukulcan – their name for Quetzalcóatl.

The Toltecs were a warlike people, who created their empire by conquest. Among their innovations was the creation of warrior orders with a common identity such as the jaguar and the eagle. Warriors were protected by small shields and wore decorative headdresses and chestplates. Like many other Mesoamerican warriors, they used the javelin propelled by an atlatl for skirmishing, with hand weapons for close-quarter combat. These included knives and maces, plus a stone-headed weapon that was somewhere between a mace and an axe.

Most of the Toltec art that survives is warlike in nature, suggesting a highly militarized society built around the warrior societies and the cult of Quetzalcóatl. The Toltecs made war for conquest but also to obtain sacrifices and to spread their religion. It is not clear how far their empire extended; there seems to have been a region they directly controlled and a wider area within which the Toltecs exerted influence and obtained tribute in the form of food, valuable goods and people to be sacrificed.

The city of Tollan, capital of the Toltec empire, is known mainly through legends and has not been positively identified.

# CHOCOLATE

THE EARLIEST KNOWN consumption of chocolate was around 1900 BC, when the Olmecs introduced a drink made from the cacao bean. Chocolate was a status symbol to the Aztecs and the Maya (and probably others too). It was drunk from specially constructed vessels designed to ensure that onlookers knew that the owner was wealthy enough to have a supply of chocolate.

Chocolate was not only a status symbol but also took on a religious meaning when it was given to high-status sacrifices before they were put to death. It was an important trade good, and since the beans were naturally fairly uniform in size they became a medium of currency. This inevitably led to counterfeiting: beans were hollowed out and refilled with less valuable material while the cacao removed could be used or sold elsewhere.

The chocolate drink popular in Mesoamerica was created by vigorous whisking and pouring from one vessel to another, creating a frothy head that was particularly relished. The modern word 'chocolate' comes from the Aztec *xocolatl*, or 'bitter water'. Apparently, the bitterness was not to everyone's taste; *xocolatl* was flavoured with a variety of substances including honey, vanilla and chilli.

LEFT: Chocolate was unknown in Europe before the discovery of the Americas, but caught on quickly. This depiction is from a French history of chocolate published in 1685.

The most likely candidate is Tula, where extensive Toltec remains have been found. These include a ceremonial district with pyramids and statues depicting Toltec warriors. The city was sacked around 1150 AD and destroyed, with the remnants further looted in later centuries. It is not clear who destroyed Tollan, but there is some evidence that the Toltec civilization might have been riven apart by civil war or a popular uprising.

The legendary conflict between Ce Acatl Topiltzin and his enemy Tezcatlipoca may reflect a discord in Toltec society. Ce Acatl Topiltzin is said to have made very few human sacrifices and instead gave his own blood, which was sufficient to appease the gods. Tezcatlipoca wanted more sacrifices and ultimately overthrew Ce Acatl Topiltzin. If this tale is symbolic of internal conflict, then perhaps a more bloodthirsty element of the priesthood tried to gain ascendance and triggered a destructive civil war.

ABOVE: The Toltecs, like many Mesoamerican cultures, revered eagles and commonly depicted them in art. Eagles were connected with shamanism and the spirit world as well as inspiring elite warriors.

Whatever the truth of this, the lands of the Toltec civilization were invaded in the 1200s by a number of warlike peoples, including the emerging Aztecs. The Toltec culture was destroyed, although elements of it were co-opted by the Aztecs or survived through cultural exchange with other societies. The Aztecs were sufficiently impressed with the Toltecs to revere them as the founders of civilization and little short of wonder-workers.

OPPOSITE: A mask depicting the complex and rather sinister god Tezcatlipoca. It was formed from a mosaic of turquoise pieces over an inner structure of the mask, which was provided by a human skull.

This reverence was one reason why so little remains of the Toltec civilization. The Aztec elite claimed to be descended from the Toltec ruling class, and sent expeditions to Toltec cities to remove artefacts and statues. Thus, much of what is known about the Toltec civilization is in fact Aztec legend about how great their ancestors were, and may be of questionable veracity.

CHAPTER 3

# The Maya Civilization

Centred in what is now Guatemala, the Maya civilization was the longest lasting of the Mesoamerican cultures. The reason for its decline remains the subject of much debate among historians, while its calendar system has been the subject of spurious doomsday predictions.

THERE IS EVIDENCE of permanent settlements in the Yucatán peninsula and nearby areas dating back to at least 2500 BC. Prior to this, the region is thought to have been inhabited for several thousand years by nomadic and later semi-nomadic people. At least some of these groups of people practised a form of slash-and-burn agriculture, clearing an area for temporary use and using the ashes as a form of fertilizer.

Experience indicated which plants provided the best return in terms of food for a given amount of effort, and by 2500 BC maize was being grown in some areas. Increased skill as farmers allowed the people of the region to settle in one place on a more or less permanent basis. Hunting still formed an important part of food production until the domestication of turkeys provided a manageable meat-producing resource. There is no evidence of

OPPOSITE: **With complex art that seems strange – alien, even – to the Western eye, the Mayan civilization was a prime candidate for spurious claims about 'lost secrets of the ancients'. Their calendar, in particular, has given rise to some distinctly oddball theories.**

ABOVE: Discovered in 1895 as part of a row of eight stelae at Piedras Negras in Guatemala this carving was once richly painted in red, green and blue, though only traces of the colours now remain.

this before around 300 BC, however; until this time, hunting parties provided most of the meat eaten by the proto-Maya.

The move to a sedentary lifestyle based upon farming happened earlier in the south where the soil was more fertile, and gradually spread north into the Yucatán peninsula from around 800 BC. Living in the lowlands, there was little need to develop exotic farming methods such as raised fields, nor to build complex irrigation canal systems such as were necessary in some other regions. Eventually, the whole population was supported by agriculture, growing maize and beans, and the possibility of an organized society arose.

At this time, there was no central authority, just a scattering of villages whose people presumably had common cultural values as a result of living in the same environment and trading with one another. They spoke a common language, referred to as Proto-Mayan. In time, some of their villages grew into city-states, but the Maya were never a unified society as such. There was no Mayan empire ruled over by a single central authority; instead, the Maya are best thought of as a loose federation of smaller states sharing common traits.

Conflict was not uncommon between the proto-Maya states, although there do not appear to have been large-scale wars of conquest. Trade, cooperation or at least coexistence was the norm, and ideas were passed between the early Mayan settlements along with goods and religious beliefs. A general trend towards larger communities requiring greater organization eventually led to the rise of an identifiably Mayan culture.

# THE MAYAN LANGUAGE

AROUND 2000 BC, THE ancestors of the Maya spoke a common language now referred to as Proto-Mayan. This diverged over time into multiple subgroups, but at some point the beginnings of a written language began to appear. The earliest surviving examples of Mayan writing date from around 250 BC, but the origins of a written form have been suggested to be much earlier – perhaps 500 years or more.

Mayan writing was complex, with some glyphs representing syllables, and others whole words, concepts and names of places and gods. It was carved into stonework but also written on softer materials such as bark. It is probable that the written form of the language was 'classic Mayan', which was used by officials and perhaps merchants but that was not spoken on a daily basis by most people.

BELOW: The surviving Mayan codices are named for the cities where they are held; it is not known what the authors named them.

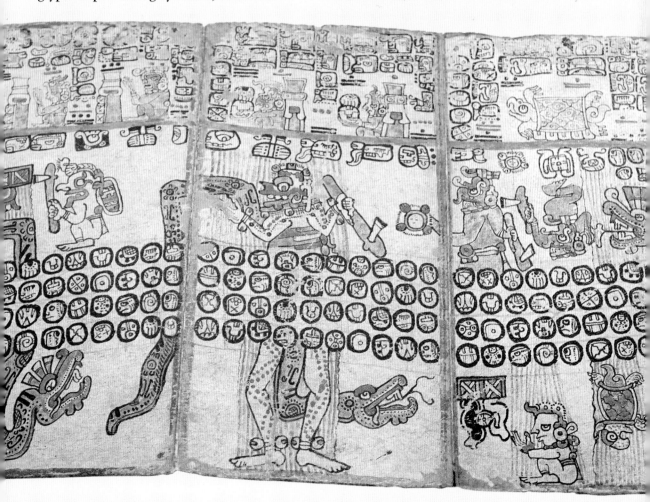

## THE RISE OF THE CITIES

The Mayan population was spread over a large area with differing terrain. The lowlands of the north, mostly within the Yucatán peninsula, lay between the Gulf of Mexico and the Caribbean Sea, but received relatively low rainfall and were less agriculturally productive than the lands to the south. The Guatemalan highlands to the south were cooler and more fertile, though occasionally affected by volcanic activity. Between the two was another area of lowlands, forming the third major division of Mayan territory.

The different conditions in these major regions and many subregions contributed to the evolution of multiple languages

BELOW: This reconstruction of the site at Dos Pilas shows aspects of the Mayan religion – a ceremony atop the temple pyramid watched by the general populace, whilst a ceremonial ball game is in progress.

within the Mayan language family, and to the uneven spread of cultural traits as well as limit technologies. The people of the Guatemalan highlands are often referred to as the K'iche' Maya for their main language group, while those living in the Yucatán peninsula are typically called Yucatec Maya. These distinctions are very broad, of course; there were significant variations in language, beliefs and customs across quite short distances.

ABOVE: San Bartolo became an important centre for trade and culture in the Late Pre-Classic period. The oldest known Mayan murals have been found there, along with numerous carvings depicting gods and cosmology.

The growth of early Maya settlements depended first and foremost on the availability of food, then on good leadership that could mitigate the inevitable setbacks and disasters that would occur in the lifetime of any community. Those that weathered difficult times in relative stability had a chance to grow into large towns and finally cities.

The potential importance of any given city depended largely upon trade. Physical isolation due to difficult terrain might enhance security but ultimately limited the influence a city could exert as well as limit access to goods that could not be sourced locally. Political isolation arising from bad relations with other cities would have the same effect.

In the longer term, those cities that joined the emerging trade network and maintained at least neutral relations with their neighbours prospered and continued to grow. As the cities grew larger, trade became ever more important and those that controlled it benefited the most. Often this was an accident of geography, with some cities standing on important trade routes and becoming the hubs of commerce.

Over time, some cities began to build roads and causeways to their neighbours. These may have had religious significance, but they certainly made trade easier and more efficient. Political advantage was also gained from more rapid and regular

# MAYAN CITY LAYOUTS

UNLIKE CULTURES IN OTHER parts of Mesoamerica, the Maya did not build their cities on a neat grid pattern. This has less to do with continual occupation and building over of earlier structures than with what lay beneath them. In most cases, the Maya were constructing their settlements on damp and uneven ground, and had to build wherever firm and dry foundations could be laid.

As a result, a Maya city typically resembles an uneven cluster of large and small plazas, each surrounded by buildings and often linked to other plazas by a raised causeway. The central plazas are large and contain ceremonial buildings such as pyramids, temples and ball courts, while those further from the centre are smaller and more mundane.

communication, enabling a city to obtain assistance at need or to benefit from the misfortune of others by timely action.

For many years, modern scholars believed that the cities of the Maya were not inhabited as such. They were instead thought to be ceremonial centres, with the population dwelling elsewhere and visiting only for important rites. A small community of priests and those who supported them would be the only permanent residents. It is now known that this was not the case; the cities took a dispersed form, with most of the population dwelling outside the ceremonial centre, but not far enough away to be considered a separate community.

The pattern of most Mayan cities is similar, with important ceremonial buildings in the central area surrounded by residential and economic areas. This form was probably set early on in the development of Mayan culture, at a time before great works of construction could be undertaken, and continued to be followed throughout the development of the cities. Some of these communities stood in one form or another for many centuries; what had begun as a small village on a trade path eventually grew into a powerful city-state.

The earliest known Maya settlement is at Cuello, in modern Belize. Settled around 2500 BC, a sizable community existed there by 2000 BC, at the beginning of the Early Pre-Classic era of Mesoamerican history. Cuello is known to have produced pottery of an unusual style known as Swasey. This is the earliest use of ceramics in the region that has been discovered to date, and may suggest that pottery was invented independently in this area rather than being introduced from an outside source.

Cuello was inhabited into the Classic period of the Maya culture, as late as 500 AD, with structures rebuilt or built over during that time. As a rule, the most important buildings and the homes of the most influential citizens were constructed on the highest ground, with ordinary people taking what was left over. A home that became dilapidated might be demolished and rebuilt many times, while some plots might be too prone to subsidence or flooding to be viable in the longer term. As a result, it was the more grand and important buildings that survived to be found by modern archaeologists, creating the

BELOW: The Maya city at Xunantunich in modern Belize grew from an unimportant village into a major community during the Late and Terminal Classic phases, whilst other parts of the Maya civilization were in decline.

BELOW: Art pervaded Mayan society; pieces were produced on a large scale by specialist groups or individually by expert artists. Most surviving pieces are sculptures or carvings, or else ceramics.

false impression that Mayan cities were not dwelling-places but served a ceremonial function only.

## OUTSIDE INFLUENCES

From 1200 BC or so, the Olmec civilization began to flourish to the west of what would become Mayan territory. The main Olmec centres lay close to the Gulf of Mexico coast, but the Olmecs were influential over a much wider area. Their influence was strongest along the Pacific coast of what are now Mexico, Guatemala and El Salvador, but their traders reached the emerging Mayan villages and imparted ideas and beliefs.

The Olmec civilization was diminished after 900 BC, with the destruction of San Lorenzo, but trade continued with other Olmec centres. The communities of the Maya were at the time small, and may have found it more convenient to bring in goods from the more developed Olmec cities than to try to develop their own production. The Olmecs wanted raw materials such as jade and feathers, and staple items such as pottery and food. In return they offered finished goods – often made from the materials they imported.

As the Maya towns grew into cities, it became possible to manufacture more finished goods within Maya territory, but the Olmecs continued to be an important part of regional culture until La Venta was destroyed. This event coincides with the beginning of the Late Pre-Classic period in Mesoamerican history.

The Maya learned much from the Olmecs but developed a distinctive culture of their own. They used the same base 20 counting system as the Olmecs, and their calendar incorporated the Olmec dating system. Mayan art developed its own distinctive style; in particular, the Maya were skilled at creating different colours and tones of paint that could survive in their tough environment.

Mayan society was stratified, but not to such an extent as in many other cultures. The upper echelons included military leaders and religious figures, supported by a large skilled middle class. Middle-class occupations included warriors, merchants and engineers as well as administrators and civic officials. Below these strata were the agricultural and unskilled workers, who had a degree of social mobility and were able to enter the middle classes through talent and hard work.

For the ordinary folk, life revolved around an extended family that formed part of a group of families who were likely to be related by a common ancestor. Men undertook tasks such as construction or maintenance of the buildings, along with agriculture and hunting. Until the domestication of the turkey, the Maya relied on hunting to provide meat, and since areas close to the city were unlikely to have much game, hunting parties might be gone for several days at a time.

Agriculture developed from the original planting of whatever land was suitable, to extensive slash-and-burn projects. More technical methods included the creation of chinampas much like those used elsewhere. This was a major undertaking at first, but

ABOVE: Some Mayan murals have survived to the present, such as this example found at Cacaxtla. The mural depicts the city's importance as a trade centre as well as religious and battle scenes.

BELOW: El Mirador forms part of the Labna archaeological site in Mexico. The lattice atop the main structure is a roof comb, presumably added to increase the already imposing height of the building.

once established a raised-field system could be maintained by a smaller number of workers. No single housing complex could carry out such a large building project alone; the creation of chinampas and their associated water-management systems were overseen by the ruling class.

Adult women ran the household and undertook most tasks within it, such as cooking, making ceramics and weaving clothes, and grew vegetables and fruit in plots close to the housing complex. Children assisted with various tasks depending on their age and capabilities, often being assigned to look after animals. Within a city, each cluster of dwellings occupied by a group of

families was a self-contained community that could provide for most of its own needs.

Perhaps as a result of their social organization, the Maya made rapid progress in technology and techniques for using it. Over time, they developed more effective forms of agriculture including irrigation techniques and the use of terracing. Early in the development of Mesoamerican society, when populations were small, simple farming techniques were sufficient to support a village, but as cities grew the Maya had to improve their food production to keep pace.

Perhaps as a result of their social organization, the Maya made rapid progress in technology and techniques for using it.

By 300 BC, the Mayan social order was well established, along with the concept of hereditary positions. The earliest great construction works were also undertaken around this time, marking the beginning of the Late Pre-Classic period. Mayan pyramids were aligned with astronomical and seasonal phenomena such as solstices and, like other Mesoamerican pyramids, were of stepped construction. Representations of the classic Mayan gods were carved into these early monumental structures, though not always in their classical form. This suggests that some aspects of Mayan culture were still developing during the Late Pre-Classic period.

## THE PROTO-CLASSIC PERIOD

The pattern for the development of the Mayan city-states is familiar; among a cluster of villages, one or more grew to become a hub or local capital for the others. These towns attracted trade and talented people who gradually became a ruling elite over the region. As the towns became cities, they expanded further and social stratification became more apparent. The Mayan civilization

ABOVE: **The La Danta pyramid complex was constructed, like many monumental structures, in a series of stages which modified and built on (or over) the previous work, gradually expanding into one of the largest structures in the ancient world.**

had reached its classic form by around 250 AD, although some areas lagged behind in development.

Between the Late Pre-Classic period and the Early Classic is an interval of around 150 years known as the Proto-Classic. One of the cities that flourished during this period is now known as El Mirador. El Mirador lies in a natural basin in northeastern Guatemala that has incredible biodiversity. Its fertile wetlands provided sustenance for the expanding city, which reached a population of 100,000 or more from 200 BC to 150 AD.

El Mirador dominated the surrounding area and was a major trade hub. It is thought to have been the largest of the Mayan city-states for a time, and certainly was one of the earliest very large cities. It is the site of the La Danta pyramid complex, one of the largest in the world. La Danta was built on and around a low hill, with several platforms rising above the jungle floor. These supported temples, plazas and other structures, with the highest platform topped by three pyramids.

If the La Danta pyramid complex were to be considered a single structure then it would be one of the largest buildings ever constructed. However, its platforms were built over time and make use of natural terrain features. Thus, although La Danta has a claim to being the largest construction project undertaken by the Mayan civilization, it is not the largest pyramid they built.

Nearby is the El Tigre pyramid complex. From the top of these two complexes it is still possible to see the remains of other cities where their pyramids poke through the jungle canopy. Causeways, known as sacbe, or 'white roads', lead from

El Mirador to these other cities and beyond. Many have been lost over time, but the 40-km (25-mile) causeway to El Tintal and the 12-km (7-mile) route to Nakbe have survived to be excavated in modern times.

The sacbeob (plural of sacbe) were built as elevated causeways rising as much as 6m (20ft) from the wet jungle floor and were at least 20m (66ft) wide. They were more than simply a means of transport. The sacbeob also helped control flooding and water movement. They were important to trade and politics, and there are varying theories about their spiritual significance. It is likely that going to a city for a major ceremony was considered a pilgrimage, in which case the roads travelled would have

BELOW: **The Ornate Palace at Labna is named for its intricate decoration. Its outer walls are covered with glyphs and patterns connected with Mayan cosmology. The palace also features a large carved representation of the rain-god, Chac.**

# THE MAYAN CALENDAR

THE EARLIEST KNOWN EXAMPLES of the Mayan calendar date from around 400 BC. It was created by adding additional dating systems to the existing Olmec solar calendar. The latter was the 'civil calendar' of the Mayans, dividing the year into 18 months of 20 days plus five additional days. It was of great importance to farmers and those whose endeavours depended on weather conditions such as merchants trading with far-off cities.

To the Haab, or civil calendar, the Maya added a second dating system, called Tzolk'in in Yucatec Mayan. This was the 'sacred calendar', subdivided into thirteen cycles of 20 days. Various reasons have been suggested for this choice, including the time from conception to birth of a human child and a more abstract nine lunar months, or perhaps a connection to growing cycles.

The interaction of these two cycles was significant to the Maya. Every single day in a 52-year cycle could be uniquely identified with its names from the Haab and Tzolk'in calendars, and a person who had lived through an entire cycle was considered to be an elder and therefore wise. For time spans greater than a calendar cycle, the Long Count was used instead. This uses similar building blocks to Western calendars – days, months and years, for example – but in different proportions.

The Long Count calendar was created by people who used base 20 rather than base 10, and reflects this.

- The basic unit is named 'kin' and is one day long.
- Twenty days make a month in both the civil and sacred calendars, named 'uinal'.
- Eighteen months make a year in the Long Count, since 18 x 20 is closer to a Haab year of 365 days than 20 x 20 would be. A year is named 'tun' and is 360 days long.
- Twenty years makes a 'katun', or 7200 days.
- Twenty katun makes a 'baktun' of 144,000 days.

The Long Count operates in a Great Cycle of 13 baktun, or approximately 5125 years, within which any date can be uniquely identified by the number of baktun, katun, tun, uinal and kin that have elapsed since the beginning of the cycle. The current Great Cycle began in December 2012; the one before it in August 3114 BC.

The end of the previous Great Cycle was the subject of a number of end-of-the-world predictions, all based upon the idea that the ancient Maya somehow knew that the world would end on a particular date and based their calendar on it. There do not seem to be any Maya doomsday legends, nor anything to suggest that they believed the world would perish at the end of the Great Cycle, but the idea got into the popular consciousness by way of movies and modern-day doomsayers. They do not appear to have been correct.

significance as part of the endeavour. Indeed, they may have been considered holy, in that they allowed the people to reach the great temples and thus commune with their gods. Surviving records are patchy and at times contradictory, however.

The heyday of El Mirador ended around 150 AD, during the Proto-Classic period. The city's population dropped sharply and there may have been a complete, if temporary, abandonment. People drifted back to the site later, but El Mirador never regained its previous importance. It was finally abandoned around 900 AD and was never reoccupied.

## MAYAN PYRAMIDS

The ancient Mayas might have learned to build pyramids from the Olmecs, or got the idea from them and figured out how to do it by trial and error. Their pyramids were stepped, and were mostly temples, although some were burial-places for kings. Most pyramids were working buildings, but a proportion were intended to stand untouched once completed.

Those pyramids that were intended for regular use as temples typically had two or four staircases giving relatively easy access to the top. This was a flat area used for religious ceremonies and sacrifices. In many cases, there were platforms partway up the pyramid. Rituals were performed at these platforms as the priests ascended, forming part of a greater ceremony. However, not all pyramids were temples. Some were funerary monuments and not intended as sites for religious ceremonies. These typically had no staircase or a rudimentary one.

Many of the temple-pyramids were built as part of complexes with more than one temple. One example of this

BELOW: Carved in stone, Mayan calendars like this one on display in San Miguel Fort in Campeche Mexico, have survived relatively intact. The same 260/365-day dating cycle was used by the Aztec empire.

RIGHT: The people of Tikal went about their daily business with the temples of their gods towering over them. During ceremonies they would observe bound sacrifices tumbling down the long staircase to a grisly death.

survives at Tikal. There are three temples facing the pyramid, each positioned to align with the rising sun on a different solstice or equinox.

Many of the monumental buildings in Mayan territory are constructed to be in alignment with astronomical features such as the Sun, the Moon or Venus at critical times of the year. As with many societies, religious ceremonies were performed to ensure good harvests, plenty of rain, minimal flooding and other desirable circumstances. A ceremony on the right day, at a temple in alignment with the governing astronomical body, was extra potent.

The Maya believed that after death most people went to the underworld, variously named Metnal or Xibalba.

As in other Mesoamerican cultures, renewal and rebuilding was an essential part of the pyramid's life. It has been suggested that the rebuilding was scheduled to follow the 52-year cycle of the civil and holy calendars, but it is likely that the timings varied considerably. A new ruler might instigate building early – or late, if there were other matters to be dealt with first – and some pyramids seem to have been in a near-constant state of construction.

Working on any large construction project is hazardous, and given the methods of construction used for Mayan pyramids, fatalities were certain to happen during any rebuilding phase. Rather than dressed stone blocks, the typical Mesoamerican pyramid was constructed from rubble retained by walls of larger stone. Time and repeated remodelling could weaken these

# SURVIVING MAYAN RELIGIOUS BOOKS

THE K'ICHE' MAYAN HOLY text named Popol Vuh was created to preserve the ancient stories and beliefs of the Maya. The Spanish conquerors were at the time attempting to extinguish the ancient beliefs of the Mesoamerican people, and succeeded in destroying most written sources in some areas. Popol Vuh is the only holy book of the K'iche' Maya to survive, while four works of the Yucatán Maya were preserved.

Popol Vuh takes the form of an epic poem, divided into four sections by European translators but originally a single narrative from start to finish. It begins with the creation of the world and tells of the Hero Twins, Hunahpu and Xbalanque, who defeated the gods of the underworld. The tale of the creation of humans leads to an account of the ancestry of the K'iche' people of the time.

Various translations of the name Popol Vuh have been put forward. One such is 'Book of the People', although it is often called the 'Book of the Mat' for the mats used as seating when listening to tales from the book.

ABOVE: This stucco representation of the Hero Twins Huhnapu and Xbalanque was found at El Mirador.

walls, causing a partial collapse that would put nearby workers in extreme danger. Human sacrifice was an important part of Maya culture, so it is probable that these casualties were accepted – perhaps even welcomed in a way – as part of the sacred building process.

Although the details varied from place to place, the Maya believed that after death most people went to the underworld, variously named Metnal or Xibalba. The latter translates as 'place of fright', which seems apt. The underworld was home to many evil gods, some of whom occasionally got out and caused mayhem. There were also all manner of dangers: raging rivers (some of them of blood), monstrous animals, jagged mountains

OPPOSITE: Ceremonial receptacles for the heart or blood of a sacrifice usually took the form of a chacmool figure with a bowl or vase on his stomach. The term chacmool refers to a specific reclining pose with the knees drawn up and head turned.

ABOVE: The ceremonial ball game required players to pass a heavy latex ball through a circular goal without touching it with their hands. This would be difficult enough without opposing players violently attempting to prevent it.

and obsidian blades that would attack those who had to travel through this terrifying place.

To help the departed negotiate the nine levels of the underworld, friends and relatives provided funeral goods of a useful sort – tools, weapons, food and sometimes real or representational dogs. The only way to avoid going to the underworld was to be sacrificed, although it appears that at least some of the Maya believed that death in childbirth amounted to the same thing. It may be that getting killed in a rockfall while rebuilding a temple was considered a form of sacrifice, in which case relatives could take comfort in the knowledge that the victims would be spared the underworld.

## MAYAN SACRIFICES

A violent or bloody death was necessary for sacrifice, although the methods varied. Disembowelling was common for captives taken in war, while others might be executed and their hearts cut out. Whereas the Aztecs preferred to kill the victim by cutting out the living heart, the Maya typically dispatched the sacrifice by other means, then extracted the heart. Many sacrifices were not directly killed by the priests, but instead were pushed off the top of the temple-pyramid with their limbs bound, tumbling to an agonizing and messy death on the way down the long staircase.

Some sacrifices involved the ceremonial ball game. Typically, it was the losers who were ritually sacrificed afterwards, but sometimes both teams met the same fate. Winning the ball game was thus not necessarily a way to escape execution, and may not have been possible in many cases. Ball games were often played by prisoners captured after a battle, and represented a ceremonial re-enactment of the conflict. Since the ball game hosts had already won, the captives might be expected to lose the game after putting up a good fight for the sake of their souls, or might be ruled to have lost no matter what happened. Either way, captives forced to play a ball game could expect to be sacrificed – usually by beheading – afterwards.

Sometimes varying methods of sacrifice were used during a ceremony. Carvings have survived in which a ball game is taking place while sacrifices are being shoved down the pyramid stairs. At Yaxchilán, there are distinct similarities between the bound captive and the ball in play. It is likely that the ball symbolized the severed heads of enemies or sacrifices, and in some cases the ball was fashioned from an actual skull coated in rubber.

Not all sacrifices required death, even if blood was involved. For most purposes, the gods of the Maya were willing to accept

BELOW: A bas relief from the ball game court at Chichen Itza, depicting a ball with a human skull inside. Some balls used in the game were created by coating a skull with latex.

a small amount of blood from a pricked ear, penis or finger, smeared on a carving or idol, or flicked out to the cardinal points of the compass atop a temple pyramid. The blood of rulers was particularly pleasing to the Mayan deities – possibly because the ruling elite claimed to be descended from the gods – and minor bloodletting was a duty of the upper class in order to keep the gods happy.

Nobles or rulers captured in war were particularly powerful sacrifices. Not only did they represent a large quantity of noble blood to be spilled in the name of the gods, but also putting such a captive to death was a reminder of the power of a city-state and perhaps a warning to others who might oppose it.

BELOW: **The goddess Coatlicue was, like most Mesoamerican deities, complex. She was the 'earth mother' who provided food for humans but also a goddess of death and decay who took back what she gave in a never-ending cycle.**

## THE CLASSIC ERA

The classic period of the Mayan civilization began around 250 AD, and continued until around 900 AD. It is subdivided into Early and Late phases, as well as a short Terminal phase in which great upheavals took place. During the Early Classic period (250–600 AD), Mayan culture was heavily influenced by that of Teotihuacán. Goods from Teotihuacán were highly sought after by those who could afford them. Not all Teotihuacán imports could be copied locally; green obsidian only occurred in certain regions and had to be sourced externally.

For many years, modern scholars believed that the Maya were a peaceful people who had little conflict in their lives, but this is now known to be incorrect. The city-states of the Classic period warred with one another and with outside opponents,

although usually on a limited-war basis. A battle might go on for several days until one side was forced to admit defeat, typically by the loss of important warriors or leaders. Negotiations would then begin for tribute to be paid to the winner. This would include valuable goods but also prisoners who would be sacrificed at the victors' temples.

It was common to seek the assistance of one or another of the many Maya gods connected with warfare before setting out on a campaign, so a suitable sacrifice was necessary to thank the gods for their favour. Captured leaders were favoured as sacrifices, but warriors who put on a good show in the ceremonial ball game before being sacrificed were also pleasing to the gods.

ABOVE: A reconstruction of a Mayan painting of a battle scene depicting warriors in elaborate headdresses making vigorous use of spears and shields. It is likely that the volley of projectiles at the beginning of a battle left many wounded to be gathered as sacrifices.

The weapons and equipment of the Maya were similar to those of other Mesoamerican civilizations – stone-headed maces and spears, plus darts and javelins. Combat was an individual affair for the most part, with warriors skirmishing with projectiles before closing for decisive hand-to-hand action. There were no mass armies or levies for the most part, although the lower orders of society might turn out to fight in a rebellion against their own rulers. When fighting other city-states, the Maya left warfare to a small proportion of the population led by the city's king and nobles. It is not clear if this was a specialist military class or a segment of the population with military obligations in addition to their other activities.

One reason for this mode of warfare was the difficulty of mounting a campaign over any distance in the terrain of Mesoamerica. Not only did taking peasants away from their work weaken the city's economy, but also each man contributed

BELOW: The Central Acropolis at Tikal was constructed in the Late Pre-Classic period by levelling off the top of a natural rock formation as a foundation for the palace of the ruling family.

only a small amount of fighting power in return for an increased logistics burden. Supporting a force of more than a few hundred warriors over a distance of a week's march was impossible for most cities.

Some cities were fortified; others were not. Later in the Classic period, it was common to build defensive walls of earth or stone, and these were sometimes extensive. New cities tended to occupy defensive terrain such as hills, whereas the older settlements, perhaps dating from less turbulent times, were more likely to be located close to good agricultural land.

Some cities show signs of defensive works that were apparently thrown up in haste, within the city. In many cases

When fighting other city-states, the Maya left warfare to a small proportion of the population led by the city's king and nobles.

these were constructed between existing buildings to incorporate them into the defences. Rather than attempt to encircle the whole sprawling city in a defensive ring, the inhabitants seem to have concentrated their defences on key areas. Stone was at times cannibalized from existing buildings, even important ones, suggesting a desperate time in a city's history.

The best-documented war between Mayan cities took place between Calakmul and Tikal, culminating in the defeat of Tikal in 562 AD. This was the end of the Early Classic period, a time of warfare and turbulence across much of the Mayan world. While few records exist, the lack of monumental building work between 534 and 593 AD suggests that normal activity was greatly disrupted.

Tikal rose to prominence near the beginning of the Early Classic period, largely as a result of its favourable location and good natural resources. The settlement is known to date from around 300 BC, and was presumably a city of some size by 100 AD, when construction of monumental buildings began. Tikal had contact with Teotihuacán, although whether this was economic in nature or more violent is unclear. It is likely that both occurred during the city's development. Either way, Tikal was influenced by the culture of Teotihuacán to a considerable degree.

ABOVE: Captured rulers and similar high-value individuals were commonly sacrificed by pushing them down the temple stairs. The result would be to spread out the sacrifice's blood over a wide area, which was presumably pleasing to the gods.

Tikal's power grew sufficiently that it was able to conquer other cities, notably Rio Azul and Uaxactun. Outright conquest was rare in the Mayan world, although a powerful city might control others through a mix of economic dominance and the threat of military action. The city-state of Kaminaljuyu was counted among the allies of Tikal rather than its vassals, and like Tikal, Kaminaljuyu appears to have had strong links with Teotihuacán. The architecture of its monumental buildings and the design of the pottery found within them indicate strong cultural affinity.

The city of Caracol, in modern Belize, rose to prominence later than Tikal; along with other newcomers, it attempted to force its way on to the stage of history. War with Tikal ended in 562 AD with the capture of the king of Tikal, who was taken in great reverence to Caracol and treated as an honoured guest until his sacrifice to the gods. This must have pleased them greatly; Caracol continued to flourish while Tikal was greatly diminished for many years.

## THE LATE CLASSIC PERIOD

Tikal was not destroyed when it was defeated, and after 600 AD its population and power increased once more. Tikal defeated Calakmul, an ally of Caracol, in 695 and underwent a large-scale building programme in the years that followed.

Similarly, the city of Copán enjoyed a period of stability and prosperity in the 600s. Copán was an old city, built on the site of a settlement known to date from 1000 BC or earlier, although its ruling dynasty emerged much later. It is possible that the city had close links with Tikal and that some of its rulers came from there. Copán founded the city of Quirigua as a colony or daughter settlement, but the two eventually came into conflict. Copán's king was captured and sacrificed in 738 AD, after which Copán was eclipsed by Quirigua.

Perhaps the most notable of the Mayan cities in the Late Classic period was Palenque. The Mayan name for the city was Lakamha; the modern name was applied by Spanish explorers who were impressed by its fortifications (*palenque* meaning a stockade or a palisade). Palenque existed before 450 AD, but there are few records of its kings or their deeds from this period. In 615 AD, Pacal the Great became king of Palenque. Followed by his sons and their dynasty, Pacal developed Palenque into a major power.

By this time, the city was well established and most of its major features were in place. The city boasted some of the earliest corbelled ceilings in Mesoamerica and had a distinctive style that differed from most other cities, in using thinner walls. An aqueduct guided natural streams through the city to ensure a reliable supply of water.

BELOW: Pacal the Great founded the ruling dynasty that brought Palenque to prominence. His jade burial mask was among the treasures found when the Temple of the Inscriptions at Palenque was excavated.

RIGHT: The Temple of the
Sun at Palenque is one of a
group of three constructed
in the late 7th century, all
facing inwards to a central
plaza. Inscriptions on the
temples emphasize the
importance of the Pacal
dynasty as intermediaries
with the gods.

Pacal and his sons oversaw the construction of fortifications, suggesting that violence and instability were increasing at the time, and great works including several major temples. The palace begun by Pacal and finished by his descendants was one of the most impressive of all Mayan building projects, including a tower of a design unique in all of Mesoamerica. Pacal's own

tomb was a nine-layered temple. It, too, is unique in that it was begun in Pacal's lifetime specifically to be his final resting place.

The Classic period was the height of Mayan civilization, but by 800 AD a decline had begun. The reasons are not fully understood today and were probably complex. Warfare, climate change and pressure from outside cultures of increasing power may have contributed to a general weakening of the Mayan cities. It is possible that social upheaval took place, with the population rising up against their rulers in some cities.

The period 800–915 AD is sometimes termed the Terminal Classic period, although the Mayan civilization did not come to an end. Indeed, in the northern region, many cities continued to prosper, but in the central areas the construction of monumental buildings came to an end around 830 AD.

## THE DELINE OF THE MAYA
The decline of Mayan civilization is often termed a collapse, but this implies that it took place rapidly. In fact, the collapse took place over a period of 150 years. The depopulation or abandonment of cities was nothing new, but during the Terminal Classic period it took place far more commonly than before; rather than the odd city being abandoned there is evidence of whole regions being almost entirely depopulated.

The most likely explanation for the collapse is a downward spiral resulting from conflict, social unrest and natural conditions. These fed off each other, with the population losing confidence in their leaders and becoming more restive as conditions worsened. Warfare was a possible solution, not only allowing the resources of other cities to be seized but also the capture of large numbers of potential sacrifices in the hope of appeasing the gods. However, conflict drained resources that were becoming scarcer and might not be successful.

It is known that in some areas food production declined rapidly as a result of soil exhaustion. Here the Maya were victims of their own success; the intensive farming methods needed to support high-population cities were not sustainable in the longer term. The repeated failure of previously reliable

OPPOSITE: This relief from Palenque depicts Pacal ascending the throne. The kneeling figure is probably a captive or a defeated enemy, who no doubt will meet a grim fate at the hands of the new emperor.

ABOVE: The Temple of Kukulcan stands at the centre of Chichen Itza on the Yucatán Peninsula. The city flourished in the Late Classic period and was still important well into the Post-Classic period.

crops must have seemed like divine disfavour, although no amount of human sacrifices seemed sufficient to remedy the situation.

Warfare also seems to have become more savage. Whereas previously it was the norm to fight a limited conflict and negotiate tribute to settle the matter, it seems that cities were being destroyed or crippled by losses. Perhaps this was due to an inability to pay suitable tribute, which was both a symptom and a cause of further decline. Drought, earthquakes and plagues were other possible causes, although the Mayan civilization had weathered these before.

As the Terminal Classic period continued, the greater city-states lost control over their vassals and outlying territories, or had to engage in costly wars to keep them. Those wars, of course, diminished the value of the holdings they retained, continuing the downward spiral. New centres of power began to appear, challenging the established order for dominance or simply survival.

By 1000 AD or so, the central lowlands had been all but depopulated. It is known that a series of droughts occurred, but this alone would not be sufficient to destroy the Mayan civilization. There was no single cause, but the final factor was disaffection among the general populace. The most important duty of the nobility was to appease the gods and thus keep the rains coming. Amid chronic drought and famine, it must have appeared to the general populace that their kings and nobles had failed them and were no longer capable of serving their purpose. Total collapse of the social order followed and with it any chance of weathering the hard years.

## THE POST-CLASSIC PERIOD

Although the Mayan civilization collapsed by 1000 AD, it did not entirely disappear. The northern region suffered less than elsewhere and retained a recognizably Mayan culture into the Post-Classic period. The city of Chichen Itza, in the north of the Yucatán peninsula, was founded before 600 AD and continued to grow in importance as other cities declined.

Chichen Itza seems to have grown rapidly as a result of population migration from the south. These people were possibly displaced as a result of the collapse taking place elsewhere, and may have been very diverse. Thus, the parts of the city that were constructed during this period reflect influences from all over the Mayan world. This part of the city is named 'Old Chichen'.

BELOW: Constructed in the Terminal Classic period, the Temple of Kukulcan is an example of the ultimate development of Mayan monumental architecture. Counting the temple level itself, the steps of its four staircases add up to 365.

From around 950 AD onwards, Chichen Itza began to display influences of the Toltec civilization, with new structures built in a Toltec style. It is possible that the city received an influx of people after the destruction of Tula, increasing the Toltec influence still further.

Chichen Itza came to dominate its region, creating what might be considered the nearest thing to a 'Mayan empire' to exist. This was not without opposition from other cities; there is evidence of warfare and the conquest of nearby cities. Chichen Itza is likely to have benefited from the collapse taking place elsewhere. Any city that could remain stable during these difficult times would experience a trade bonanza as goods from other city-states became scarcer and buyers needed to locate a new source.

> By the time the first Spanish explorers arrived in the region, there was no organized Mayan state to oppose them.

However, Chichen Itza was eventually eclipsed by Mayapan, which according to legend was founded in 1250 AD by a great leader named Kukulcan. This was not the god Kukulcan but a mortal ruler who took or was given that name, creating confusion when deciphering the legends of the Maya and other Mesoamerican people who came into contact with them.

Mayapan rose as Chichen Itza declined and ultimately conquered its rival, but never achieved the glory of earlier city-states. However, its people were still able to build monumental structures that show distinct influences of the Toltec-Maya culture at Chichen Itza. The city

OPPOSITE: The observatory at Mayapan assisted in predicting agricultural seasons using the movements of Venus. The Maya also believed that the position and movement of stars and planets had religious significance.

was destroyed around 1450 AD, possibly due to an epidemic or
natural disaster that weakened it beyond the point of recovery.
As Mayapan was the last great Maya city, its destruction marked
the end of a long-lived civilization.

By the time the first Spanish explorers arrived in the region,
there was no organized Mayan state to oppose them, but
remnants of the old city-states still existed. The Maya resisted the

# MAYAN STELAE AND WRITING

STELAE ARE UPRIGHT STONE slabs carved with images and hieroglyphic writing. Many were erected in honour of kings, and in some cases are the sole surviving record of a ruler and his deeds. In many cases, all we know about a king or god is what can be gleaned from such carvings. For this reason, some kings and deities are known by peculiar-sounding names like '7 Death' because their name is written with these hieroglyphs. How the name was pronounced remains a mystery.

The Mayan culture was decentralized and lasted a very long time, creating large variations in how they wrote and what symbols they used. As a result, many inscriptions remain untranslatable, and it is quite possible that some of the translations that exist contain incorrect interpretation of a glyph whose meaning changed over time.

Levels of literacy among ordinary Mayan citizens are thought to have been high, although few would have had time to carve their words into rock. Other materials were used, and books were produced using bark. These might have provided more clues to allow modern interpretation of ancient glyphs, but the vast majority were destroyed by Spanish missionaries. It is thought that the surviving codices, as they are called, were created in response to the Spanish threat to the traditional Mayan belief system and were kept hidden wherever possible. However, the missionaries thought it was their holy mission to destroy the old ways and implement their own religion, and zealously sought out these books. Only a handful are known to have survived.

LEFT: Mayan stelae are carved in an intricate and 'busy' style that would make them confusing even if there was a single system of glyphs in use.

invaders as best they could, but, weakened by disease and outmatched by the Spaniards' weapons, they ultimately succumbed. Spanish missionaries set about destroying the traditional Mayan beliefs, burning all the holy books they could find. One of the few that survived is thought to have been created in Mayapan.

The Maya themselves survived into the modern world, retaining their traditional languages and a mix of Christianity and older beliefs. Many of their great cities were lost in the jungle and have only recently been rediscovered. Pilots flying over the jungle in the 1930s saw what they thought to be volcanoes poking through the jungle canopy. On closer inspection, some of them turned out to be monumental buildings.

The remote location of many of these cities makes archaeology difficult, and there is still much that is unknown about the Mayan civilization. Much of what is commonly 'known' is distorted by popular fiction, confused by early misconceptions or else deliberately twisted to support a questionable theory about aliens or doomsday prophecies. Indeed, there are few ancient civilizations about which there is so much misunderstanding. However, a clearer picture is gradually emerging of a grand, but not unified, civilization that built great works without the wheel or even metal tools.

## MAYAN COSMOLOGY AND GODS

Mayan cosmology was similar to that of certain other cultures that they could not possibly have met. The cosmos rested on the back of a turtle, from whose shell grew Yaxche, the world tree. The tree grew through all nine levels of the underworld and the world of humans, then through the 13 levels of paradise until its branches spread out to become the Milky Way. The corners

ABOVE: A depiction of the maize god, found in the Great Plaza of Copán. The importance of maize and its associated gods is a recurring theme in Mesoamerican culture from the earliest complex societies to the great civilizations of the Maya and the Aztecs.

RIGHT: Rain gods were extremely important to Mesoamerican cultures. Foremost among them for the Maya was Chac, who struck the clouds with his axe or hurled snakes (symbolizing fertility) into them to cause thunder and rain.

BELOW: Kukulcan was one of the first gods to try to create humans. Unsuccessful efforts resulted in additional gods being brought in to help until finally a race of beings was created out of maize dough.

of the world were supported by the four Bacabs, who were wind gods. The positive and negative energies created by the four wind gods (Ix, Muluc, Kan and Cauac) were used by the other gods to power their acts of creation.

The Maya had many gods. Some were connected with important aspects of life such as rain, maize or agriculture; others with places such as a particular city-state. There was no centrally organized religion; different regions had variations on the myths and legends or called gods by other names. Some areas had gods that did not exist elsewhere, or did not recognize deities common in other regions. A citizen of one Mayan city would usually be able to recognize the gods of another, and would be familiar with the general text of a story about them even if their version featured a different number of gods or unfamiliar details.

The Mayan gods were powerful beyond the understanding of humans, but manifested themselves in ways that could be understood. Some were represented by natural forces such as rain or thunder; some by creatures or places. In keeping with the Mayan belief in cycles of constant change, the nature of any given god could alter over time. The gods were not perfect, or immortal, and they needed to feed to survive. In this way, the Mayan gods were at once creatures of the earth and forces of the cosmos.

Serpents, or creatures with some of the features of a serpent, are common in Mayan carvings. Many gods are depicted as a combination of more than one creature, such as Kukulcan. Kukulcan has been described as the prototype for the Aztec god Quetzalcóatl, a feathered serpent with great powers, and may have been based on an Olmec deity. As with many Mayan gods, Kukulcan is known by other names in different regions. The K'iche' version is Gukumatz.

The story of Gukumatz survives in the holy book of the K'iche' Maya, the Popol Vuh, but there is less information on Kukulcan. It is thus not possible to say whether the deeds of Kukulcan were the same as those of Gukumatz – which, given the local variations in mythology to which the Maya were prone, would not rule out them being the same god.

Kukulcan is credited with being one of the creator gods who made humans. As always, there are different accounts, with varying numbers of gods involved. The gods' intent was to create a race of beings who would worship them, but their first attempt produced animals instead. Animals were not smart enough or too unruly to provide proper respect, so they were relegated to a lower place in the cosmic order.

The gods tried again and made humans out of clay. When these people crumbled away, the creator gods wondered what

BELOW: The concept that humans were created from maize makes sense; it was the staple food of the Mayan civilization. The corn god, depicted here, required a return of the favour in the form of bloodletting.

had gone awry. They rallied the support of additional deities, among them Xumucane and Xpiayoc. These were very ancient beings, wiser than the other gods, and they advised that clay was not a suitable material.

According to the sacred calendar, wood might be a better option than clay, so the gods created another set of humans out of wood. Wooden people did not dissolve when it rained but turned out to be unsatisfactory as they had insufficient will and intellect to revere their gods. The gods caused a great flood to get rid of the faulty humans before making a fourth and successful attempt using maize dough provided by Xumucane.

## TREPHINATION AND SKULL ALTERATION IN MESOAMERICA

THE PRACTICE OF TREPHINATION – removing part of the skull as a surgical procedure – was used for a variety of medical purposes. By relieving pressure inside the skull, it was hoped that a variety of mental and physical disorders, ranging from epilepsy to various forms of insanity, could be treated. The operation does not require particularly sophisticated tools. Evidence has been found in European Neolithic sites of patients who underwent the procedure – in some cases more than once – and survived for many more years.

Evidence exists of trephination carried out in the territory of the Maya from the Late Classic through the Post-Classic period. However, study of the practice in Mesoamerica is complicated by a number of factors. Some Mesoamerican cultures altered or mutilated the skulls of living subjects for cultural or ritual purposes; some made holes in the skulls of enemies to display them. It is also possible that what appears to be a case of trephination might actually be the removal of broken bone in a life-saving procedure after a major head injury.

The alteration of skull shape by the Maya is more easily investigated as the practice was well established and prevalent by the time European explorers reached the area. According to the Maya, they were instructed by their gods to alter the shape of their skulls to appear noble and handsome. This was achieved by binding the heads of infants and young children to guide their development into the desired shape. The process was very painful; some children died and others developed splits in the skin on the side of their heads. The process began just days after birth, and two main methods were used. One was to strap the child into a bed-like frame and apply pressure by way

Xumucane and Xpiayoc thus became the progenitors of all humanity and continued to be revered; Xumucane as the patron of childbirth and Xpiayoc as the arranger of marriages.

Kukulcan, at least in his aspect as Gukumatz, was an extremely powerful god. In addition to power over the elements he was also the tutor of humanity. From Gukumatz, humans learned how to farm and hunt, to build and to write. Gukumatz taught humans the need for laws and how to make wise ones, laying the foundations for the entire Mayan civilization. He came from the sea and went back there when his work was done, promising to return to his people in the future. Although

of boards tied to the sides of the subject's head. This later caused erect deformation, with the skull deformed upwards. Oblique deformation, creating a skull elongated at the back, was achieved by strapping paddleboards to the infant's head without immobilizing the subject in a frame.

There is some question about when and where these methods were used. Erect deformation appears to have begun around 500 BC, during the Middle Pre-Classic period, and continued into the Classic period. Oblique deformation was less common and appeared later, during the Classic period. Skull deformation was linked

RIGHT: This male skull discovered in Peru has both been modified (during early infancy) and trephinated.

to social standing, although there is some debate about exactly what each type – and the variants within the general class of oblique deformation – signified.

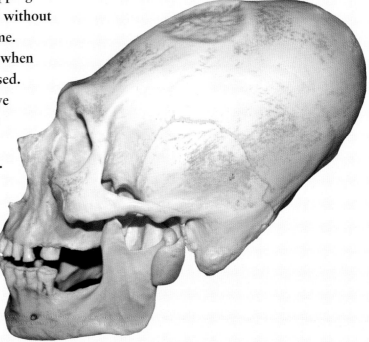

Kukulcan was favoured by the Maya as he gave them so much, he was not the greatest of their gods. Hunab-Ku is given that distinction, although there is some controversy as to when his worship began. It was claimed that Hunab-Ku was ancient and eternal, but his similarity to the Christian god suggests that he was inserted into the Mayan pantheon as a result of Spanish influences. Hunab-Ku is a distant and invisible god, although his son Itzamna is also an aspect of Hunab-Ku. Itzamna is credited, like Kukulcan, with teaching humans how to be civilized. His gifts to humanity included art and sculpture, and science and medicine. He is also the creator of the sacred calendar.

Not all of the Mayan gods were kind to humanity. Some seem to have been indifferent, as natural forces in the universe, and some were inimical. Among them was Hapikern, a great serpent that encircled the world; the brothers Yantho, Uyitzin and Usukan, who used earthquakes to harm humanity; and Tlacolotl, a god of evil and everything connected with it. Like other inimical deities, these gods were associated with the underworld.

Even the gods found the underworld daunting, and could be harmed by its denizens. The tale of the Hero Twins begins with their father (Hun Hunahpu, the maize god) and their uncle playing a riotous ceremonial ball game that disturbed the gods of the underworld. The two were summoned to Xibalba, the underworld. They were tested and tormented by the underworld gods. After being forced to cross rivers of blood and climb over spikes the two were made to play a ball game. Hun Hunahpu and his brother were defeated and subsequently sacrificed.

The bodies of Hun Hunahpu and his brother were buried under the ball court,

BELOW: Complex Mayan carvings can be interpreted in a variety of creative ways. This is an example of one claimed to represent some kind of astronauts or interplanetary travellers.

# MAYAN SPACE GODS?

INTERPRETATION OF ANCIENT MAYAN carvings can be complex, partly for stylistic reasons and partly because a given feature does not always represent exactly the same thing. Among the more controversial hypotheses is the idea that some carvings represent spaceships and astronauts. This has been illustrated by images of the relevant carvings with the lines that support the concept enhanced and others downplayed or edited out.

Combining creatively interpreted carvings with Mayan myths and the Long Count calendar has enabled various claims about Atlantis and a lost worldwide uber-civilization to be 'proven', at least to the satisfaction of those who want to believe that sort of thing. It has also been used as supporting evidence – 'evidence' in the loosest possible sense, of course – that the ancient Mayan gods came from outer space.

It is true that the Maya were interested in astronomy, but this was because the movements of planets and constellations indicated the change of seasons and the correct times to plant and reap. Likewise, they were clearly impressed with the Milky Way, but this was for no stranger reason than it is indeed very impressive in the sky above.

There is no indication that the ancient Maya were visited by spacemen. They were not taught to write or count the days by aliens, and they did not need to be shown how to farm or predict the movement of the planet Venus. Their achievements were their own, and are all the more impressive for that.

though Hun Hunahpu's head was placed on display in a tree. There, he attracted the affection of a daughter of one of the underworld gods, who somehow became pregnant with twins. These were Hunahpu and Xbalanque, the Hero Twins.

The twins were summoned before the gods of the underworld and subjected to trials and tests like their father and uncle had been, after which they too were forced to play a ceremonial ball game. Despite winning the game, the twins were to be put to death anyway, and tried to escape by jumping into a fire. The lords of the underworld brought them back, only for the twins to go on a rampage through their lands, resurrect their dead father and escape with treasures and women in a canoe.

# CHAPTER 4

# The Inca Civilization

The Inca empire existed for a relatively short period of time, but during its one-hundred-year span it grew to encompass a vast area of South America. Indeed, the Inca empire may have been the largest single state in the world at the time of its existence.

T HE INCA EMPIRE BEGAN as a particularly successful small kingdom, not dissimilar to other cultures that had arisen in the Andean Cordillera. Its initial holdings lay around Cusco in the southeast of what is now Peru. The founders of the city of Cusco were the Killke, an indigenous tribe, whose proto-state began to flourish as other powers in the region such as the Sican and Wuari cultures were in decline.

The heartland of the kingdom of Cusco lay at high altitude, around 3400m (11,150ft) above sea level, with a dry and generally temperate climate. The difficulties of producing sufficient food in this environment had been encountered by previous cultures, and Cusco undoubtedly benefited from their experience. Its society was capable of large-scale collective effort at least as early as 1100, when the grand structure known as Sacsayhuamán was constructed.

OPPOSITE: **Pachacuti (or Pachacutec) was the ninth Inca, or ruler, of his people, but the first to hold sway over an empire. He was forced by circumstances to expand his territory through conquest, leading the Inca to greatness out of necessity.**

Sacsayhuamán has been described as a fortress, and certainly would present a formidable obstacle to an attacker, but its function might not have been wholly military. At its centre was a circular structure that is believed to be a calendar based on the movements of the sun. The 'fortress' may have been used for ritual purposes as well as defence, and it possessed a large water reserve and buildings that could serve as strongpoints at need.

The fortress of Sacsayhuamán was surrounded by a triple concentric wall constructed of dressed stone. Creating it was an enormous undertaking, requiring stone blocks to be brought from quarries at least 14km (9 miles) away. Without wheeled conveyances or suitable beasts of burden, this would be difficult enough on the flat, but the altitude of the fortress required the blocks to be moved uphill from their quarries.

The stones of the walls were precisely dressed, in a manner characteristic of Inca construction. They fit together so tightly

BELOW: The concentric stone walls of Sacsayhuamán certainly give the impression of a fortress, but its actual function is open to some debate. It was constructed by the predecessors of the Inca empire, at Cusco.

that even without mortar the walls have stood for more than 500 years. The skill required to cut the blocks was considerable; even more remarkable is the fact that these huge stones were lifted into place without advanced machinery. Many of the blocks are estimated to weigh over 100 tons, prompting speculation about how the Incas and their ancestors manhandled them into place.

The stones fit together so tightly that even without mortar the walls have stood for more than 500 years.

The construction of the fortress at Sacsayhuamán is evidence that Cusco was home to a highly organized society by 1200 AD. However, there were other emerging states in South America at the time, any of which could have become a great empire. It is not clear how the kingdom of Cusco became the empire of the Incas. Perhaps Cusco was strengthened by the absorption of people arriving from elsewhere; perhaps it was

BELOW: The salt evaporation ponds at Maras were created by the Chanapata culture between 200–900 AD. After flooding a pond, it is left to evaporate in the dry mountain air, extracting salt and minerals deposited millions of years ago.

overrun but remained sufficiently intact that the conquerors could build on its strengths. All that can be discerned with any clarity is that Cusco was the birthplace of the Inca empire and remained its capital, although the people we today refer to as the Incas were culturally different from the builders of Cusco.

## THE CITY OF CUSCO

Cusco was more than a political and economic capital; it was also a symbol of the Inca way of life and the centre of their spiritual existence. It has been claimed that the city was deliberately constructed in the shape of a puma, although this is debatable. Cusco had an upper and a lower section, reflecting social divisions, while each of the sections contained four quarters

corresponding to the four parts of the Inca empire.

The upper echelons of society across the empire were concentrated in Cusco, and with them the supporting industries needed for commerce and religion. This was in part to reduce the possibility of revolt, since leaders of the more distant parts of the empire were required to live in Cusco with their families. Not only were those families hostages of a sort, but frequent and regular contact between the regional leaders and the rulers of the empire served as a constant reminder of the power of the emperor. It also made it much easier to spy on the regional rulers, and prevented them building a power base loyal first and foremost to themselves and to the empire second, if at all.

ABOVE: After the Spanish conquest, many Inca structures were destroyed or built over. The lower levels of the Qoricancha temple were used to support a Christian cathedral, symbolically claiming the site for Western religion.

Cusco was also a centre for education, ensuring that the best and brightest were not only educated to the highest possible standard but also received a thorough indoctrination with the right cultural values. These were the future leaders and administrators of the empire; guiding their education was a potent tool in ensuring future stability.

Religion lay at the heart of the Inca empire, and of their capital city too. The most important temple in the whole empire was the Qoricancha, or Golden House. Probably constructed in the 1200s, the Qoricancha lay at the meeting point of the four great highways connecting the parts of the empire. It was constructed out of dressed stone rather than the more usual irregular stonework.

The Qoricancha temple complex had four main chambers, each dedicated to a different god, and housed hundreds of priests. Sacred stones positioned atop nearby hills could be seen from the temple, and from their shadows the precise timing of the equinox and solstice could be calculated.

The Qoricancha was richly decorated in gold, and not surprisingly was plundered by the Spanish when they arrived. Some of the goldwork was more than decorative; there was a reflector that provided light throughout the temple complex and was positioned to illuminate a particularly holy chamber when the sun was in the correct alignment at the solstice.

It was commonplace for conquerors to build temples to their own gods atop the holy places of others. Many of the great churches and cathedrals of Europe are built over pagan holy sites. So it was at Cusco, where the Spanish built a cathedral atop the foundations of the Qoricancha. The cathedral was later destroyed by an earthquake, leaving the older stonework intact.

BELOW: The Inca empire had access to so much gold that it was little use as currency. It was instead used to decorate temples and to create religious objects such as this panel from the Qoricancha temple at Cusco.

## INCA CREATION STORIES

The first people to record the religion and stories of the Inca were Spanish explorers and missionaries. Not surprisingly, they chose to suppress much of what they learned, and the stories they did record were distorted by their own preconceptions and prejudices. The Incas themselves did not record their stories but committed them to the memory of oral historians. As a result, what modern historians know about Inca mythology is reconstructed as well as possible but has contradictions and differing versions of the same tale.

In some versions of the Inca creation story, the world was created by the god Con Tiqi Viracocha. Like many gods of Mesoamerica and elsewhere, Viracocha is associated with water. He is normally said to have emerged from

# CEQUES AND HUACAS

HUACAS WERE SITES OF **particular spiritual significance**, although their nature varied considerably. Many were natural, such as caves or waterfalls, while others were human-made. Huacas might be a great temple erected over many laborious years, or a simple stone marker. Some Spanish explorers translated 'huaca' as 'burial place', but this was a misunderstanding; some huacas were associated with the burial sites of notables but the majority were not.

Ceques were ritual pathways leading from the great temple at Cusco to the huacas. The pathways were as straight as possible but had to take into account

ABOVE: Some huacas, like the adobe pyramid complex now known as Huaca Pucllana, were built by previous cultures. Huaca Pucllana was constructed by the Lima culture, one of several minor societies in the region. It existed from 200–700 AD.

the rough Andean terrain. It is thought that the ceques provided a spiritual map of the universe, and each had a different significance. Who would use a given ceque and when was a complex matter that is not properly understood. It does seem that different huacas and their associated ceques were connected with certain times of the year and groups of people.

# INCA STONEWORK

LEFT: The 'twelve angled stone' is one of many carved into complex shapes to create a perfect fit where they are needed. It can be seen today at Hatun Rumiyoc Street in Cusco.

RATHER THAN USE REGULARLY sized blocks of stone, the Incas shaped each one to fit in its allotted place. This required an impressive degree of precision, especially when working without stone tools, but did not represent the greatest difficulty faced by Inca stonemasons. Once a block was ready, it had to be manoeuvred into position and the surrounding stonework supported, often at a considerable height.

Much has been made of the fact that Inca stonework was extremely precise – sufficiently so that blocks are a tight fit even though no mortar is used and buildings are surprisingly earthquake-resistant. The fact is that the stonework had to be that good if the building were to stay up. Once the need was understood, Inca craftsmen simply had to become skilled enough to produce the required degree of precision.

Experimentation has shown that it is entirely possible to produce fine stonework using stone tools, and to make irregularly sized stones fit together tightly. It is a laborious process, and often necessary to gauge by eye where a particular stone will best fit so that it need only be shaped a little. Although time-consuming and inefficient compared to working with regularly sized blocks, this system allows stonemasons to work with what is available rather than cutting stone to a precise size.

There may have been some spiritual significance to making what nature or the gods had provided fit together to make a solid whole; perhaps a metaphor for the Inca society as a whole. It is more likely, however, that the stonemasonry of the Incas was the result of pragmatism. They worked with what they had and learned how to build the structures they wanted. In short, there is no great mystery about how Inca stone structures are so precisely fitted. What is more difficult to explain is how the stones themselves were transported to the building site and how they were lifted into position.

Lake Titicaca, although there are alternative points of origin in some stories. He found a world in darkness, so created the sun and moon to light it.

Some elements of the Inca creation myth echo those of the Maya. Viracocha's first attempt to create humans was a failure; they were large and powerful but as dumb as the rocks he created them from. This failed experiment was disposed of with a flood, and the second attempt proved more successful. Viracocha sent most of his people out into the world to populate it, but kept a man and a woman at Cusco, which was the centre of the cosmos. The majority of the people were assembled at waterfalls, caves and rivers, and from there entered the world. As a result, these sites remained holy and were an important part of Inca religion.

In other versions of the story, the first god was Inti, the sun, who created the moon and stars. He had a son and a daughter with the moon. The children were sent to Earth to guide and teach humans. Similarly, there is an alternative version of the flood story where some people survived the flood on high ground, having been warned by their llamas. Although humans forgot the lesson they had learned and returned to the lowlands, the llamas remembered and would thereafter only live at high altitudes where a new flood could not reach them.

In some versions of the tale, Viracocha's people were disrespectful and ungrateful

BELOW: Viracocha was the creator of the other gods and the mortal world, and as such the most important of the Inca deities. Once his work of creation was done he left other gods to watch over the world and departed from it.

despite everything he had created for them. Humans were punished with a great drought, after which a new god named Pacha Kamaq appeared and turned the people into monkeys. He then created a new race of humans to inherit the Earth. Alternatively, Viracocha was attacked by people who did not recognize him. He caused a rain of fire, which convinced the people to worship him instead, and they were forgiven.

Before leaving the mortal realm, apparently forever, Viracocha taught mortals the skills they would need: agriculture, construction and lawmaking. He spent some time on Earth in disguise, observing his creation and occasionally helping his people. He then departed over the Pacific Ocean.

According to legend, the empire of the Incas was founded by Manco Cápac, who was the brother of Pacha Kamaq. Their father was Itzi, the sun god, and Manco Cápac was also venerated as a deity of fire and the sun. Manco Cápac entered the world with his brothers and sisters either through a cave or by rising up from the waters of Lake Titicaca. In most versions of the story he has a magical golden staff.

Details of the founding of Cusco and the Inca empire vary. In some versions, Manco Cápac and his siblings carved out an empire together, and recruited other leaders they encountered along the way. Other stories have Manco Cápac betrayed by his brothers, emerging victorious from a vicious fight to rule as the sole emperor.

## FOUNDING OF THE EMPIRE

According to myth, gods and humans emerged from the waters of Lake Titicaca at Tiwanaku, suggesting that the people who became the Inca had a strong connection to that culture. However,

BELOW: The Inca ruling family were believed to be the descendants of the gods. Thus this figure offers a libation to the sun god whilst drinking one himself, honouring his godly ancestors and his own divine nature.

# THE INCAS' LOST HISTORIES

THE CIRCUMSTANCES THAT LED to the creation of the Inca empire must be discerned from legend and archaeological evidence; the Incas had no written language, although they used devices to assist in record-keeping. Information was recorded in the form of oral histories learned by a specialist class of individuals, much as the Norse Skalds remembered their people's history and legends. The Norsemen had a written runic language but considered information such as history and the deeds of past rulers to be too important to entrust to writing; perhaps the Inca had a similar attitude.

An oral record-keeping system, other than in its most basic form, requires an organized society that can support a class of specialists. Disruption to society as a whole can result in records being lost forever, which is to a great extent what happened to the Inca. As a result, the stories that survived are fragmentary and sometimes contradictory.

Oral histories also require the protection of a powerful society that can resist attempts to alter the records. In their heyday, the Incas were such a state and could guarantee that the stories passed down from one record-keeper to another were correct and accurate. Once their power was broken, their conquerors, the Spanish, could influence what was remembered or extinguish some or all of the information as they pleased. With no written records to fall back upon, this amounted to an ability to expunge or alter whatever parts of history did not fit their agenda, and those stories would be lost forever.

little is known for sure. Cusco is said to have been founded by Manco Cápac, who threw his golden staff into the ground and declared the new city to be the centre of the world, but there is evidence of settlement there for hundreds or even thousands of years before the rise of the Incas.

In the early 1400s, the Cusco region was dominated by the Chanka people, who were extremely warlike and prone to great savagery – even by South American standards – towards captives. Their army marched on Cusco in 1438, intending to capture it, and initially it seemed that the people of the city could not resist their numbers or ferocity. Their leaders, Viracocha Inca and his son Inca Urco, chose to flee along with some of their people.

RIGHT: Prince Yupanqui led the successful defence of Cusco and subsequent campaign to destroy her enemies. He named himself Pachacuti, which – aptly considering his achievements – translates as 'reverser of the world' upon becoming ruler of the new Inca empire.

OPPOSITE: Manco Capac was the first ruler of the Inca people. According to legend he was given a golden staff by Inti, the sun god, which would show him where to make a home for his people.

Opposition to the Chanka was led by Prince Yupanqui, who was inspired by a vision from the sun god Inti. Leading only a small band of warriors, Yupanqui asked for help from gods and men. Messengers went to friendly states, and apparently Yupanqui's pleas were heard by the gods. According to legend, the gods turned large stones into powerful warriors – perhaps similar to the original and unsuccessful race of giants created before humans. With their assistance, the Inca were able to defeat their enemies. More prosaic sources suggest that allies came to help the Inca from other cities.

Perhaps realizing that the Chanka would keep returning unless decisively defeated, Yupanqui led a successful campaign to drive them from the Cusco valley, overrunning their holdings to create the beginnings of an empire. Upon becoming emperor, he took

MANCO CAPAC
E INCA I REI
DEL
PERU.

# INCA TOOLS

LACKING DRAUGHT ANIMALS AND much in the way of metallurgy, the Inca had to rely on manpower for their tasks. Their chakitaqlla, or stone-bladed plough, was used in a similar manner to a spade. Earth was laboriously turned over to one side, creating a furrow. Although vastly less efficient than the horse-drawn plough in use in Europe at the same time, the chakitaqlla was sufficiently effective that metal-bladed versions are still used in the Andes. Similar devices were used elsewhere, notably the Scottish highlands and islands, to deal with rock-strewn soil or rough terrain that would defeat a conventional plough. The chakitaqlla was complemented by the waqtana, a long-handled club used to smash up clods of earth turned over by the chakitaqlla. Farming was a cooperative task, with plough teams advancing up a field turning over the soil and followed by clod-busters armed with waqtanas.

Some bronze and copper tools were available, but most were made from natural materials such as bone, wood and stone. Even stoneworking was mainly performed with stone tools, splitting rocks along natural fracture lines rather than chiselling them.

The quipu was used to assist in record-keeping. A quipu consisted of cords that were knotted in patterns to signify numbers and important information. A trained user would know how to interpret the number, size and spacing of the knots, which would be incomprehensible to anyone else.

RIGHT: Felipe Guaman Poma, a nobleman of the Inca created a work entitled *El Primer Nueva Coronica y Buen Gobierno*, detailing Inca history and their way of life.

the title Pachacuti Inca Yupanqui, although he is more commonly
known as Pachacuti. This title can be translated in various ways,
meaning 'world-shaker' or 'reverser of the world', in the sense
that he would upset the status quo and create a new order.

Pressing on to the southeast, Pachacuti conquered the region
around Lake Titicaca and absorbed its people into his empire.
After this he took an administrative
role, leaving further conquest to his
brothers and son. Although they added
new lands to the Inca empire, Pachacuti
concentrated on developing the
hidden foundations of an empire – the
administrative and economic apparatus
that would ensure stability long after the
conquest was completed.

> Every person aged between
> 15 and 50 had to take their
> turn working as directed by
> the central administration.

The Incan empire was based on a system of tribute in goods
and obligations to work on behalf of the Inca. This 'labour
tax' was named mit'a, which means 'turn'. Every person aged
between 15 and 50 had to take their turn working as directed by
the central administration. This labour was used to build roads
and great monuments, but also to support those undertaking
other tasks. Workers taking their turn tended the fields of
families whose working-age members were away carrying out
other tasks or had been killed by war or sickness, ensuring that
society as a whole was not weakened by drafting labourers off
to some distant project.

## SOCIAL ORGANIZATION AND AGRICULTURE

The traditional Andean diet was, out of necessity, mostly
vegetarian. Fish and seafood were available on the coast or
within trading distance of it, and llama could be hunted or
herded for meat in the highlands. Most Inca families engaged in
subsistence farming, even if some family members had a craft or
trade to work at. However, there was a limit to what could be
grown in any given area that might create a deficient or at least
monotonous diet. This problem was solved by land allocation
and a high degree of organization.

Several related family units formed an ayllu, which owned areas of farmland worked by the kinfolk in common. Ideally, these were dispersed over different terrain and at varying altitudes, enabling a range of crops to be grown and thus varying the diet of family members. Potatoes and maize were grown at higher altitudes, and cacao in the lower areas. Vegetables included squash, peppers and cucumber. An ayllu might also grow peanuts, cashews and cotton as well as herding llama for food and hides.

The importance of food production was well understood, and the Inca had many rituals designed to ensure a good harvest. Offerings were made at water sources and when harvesting crops, and each year a sacred field was prepared personally by the emperor using a golden plough. Here the first maize of the year was planted. The importance of this ritual was such that the great temple at Cusco contained a full-size gold replica of a maize field.

Useable land was at a premium, so projects were undertaken to terrace steep slopes and drain wetlands. The Inca understood the necessity for crop rotation and regular fertilization with animal dung. Despite these measures, providing food for the growing empire was a challenge, which was met with efficiency and ingenuity. Indeed, one reason for the stability of the empire was efficient food storage and a good logistics network to enable it to be moved between regions.

RIGHT: The terraces at Moray, near Cusco, may have been used for investigation into new farming methods or potentially useful crops. Alternatively, the site may have been a 'control group' used to monitor the likely output of other areas.

Throughout the empire, vast numbers of stone storehouses enabled food reserves to be assembled. These were sophisticated constructions with provision for drainage when necessary and cooling by the wind. Their contents were recorded and monitored by administrators who used quipu to keep an accurate and up-to-date tally.

Storehouses were maintained close to population centres and on important roads. In the event of a poor harvest or similar emergency, the regional stores were used to support the population and they could be restocked from further afield. Some rulers also distributed extra food in an attempt to increase their popularity.

## ECONOMY AND SOCIAL CONTRACT

The Inca economy was extremely efficient. At its heart was the ayllu, a group of extended families working the land together and engaging in small-scale crafts. Cooperation and hard work was an ideal in Inca society; there was considerable pressure on an individual to pull their weight, and this was backed up by very heavy-handed law enforcement.

The Inca placed little monetary value on gold and silver. These metals were available in huge quantities but were prized for their beauty rather than rarity. The decorative items made from precious metals, and the effects that could be achieved by sheathing a building in gold, were valuable in an artistic, cultural

BELOW: **Ingapirca is the most northerly of all major Inca archaeological sites. Most structures were built with traditional Inca methods, but some parts of the site make use of mortar in the Cañari style.**

# INCA EATING HABITS

THE INCA PEOPLE typically ate two meals a day, which were usually boiled or roasted over a fire of wood or animal dung. The staples of these meals were maize and potatoes, which were often preserved. Common dishes included a form of porridge made from quinoa or a stew containing vegetables and flavourings including chilli. Fish and seafood might be added to these staples if available. Fresh meat was scarce, though it might be available after a successful hunt or the slaughter of farm animals on a special occasion.

An alternative was ch'arki, a form of preserved meat from which the modern term 'jerky' comes. Ch'arki was produced in a variety of ways. At higher altitudes, freeze-drying was an option, while in the lowlands salting and air-drying were common. Ch'arki was demanded as part of the taxation system, and was used to supply military expeditions or distributed to gain popularity with the people of a region. In the domestic household it was commonly cooked in stews; soldiers carried pieces of ch'arki as field rations.

The cold temperatures high in the Andes were highly suitable for freeze-drying

ABOVE: Potatoes were an important staple crop for the Inca, and could be preserved by a natural freeze-drying process to make chuño.

food; small potatoes left out for a few nights became a dehydrated food named chuño. Dried foods such as ch'arki, maize and chuño could be stored for years until needed, enabling the Inca to quickly supply a military expedition or alleviate a crisis caused by a bad harvest.

and spiritual sense, but gold or silver had no use as currency.

Taxation was in the form of goods and labour, and much of that labour was turned to ensuring that the economy did not suffer when soldiers were away on a campaign or large numbers of workers were needed for a great project. In addition to the mit'a, tax payable to the Inca, there were obligations at a more local social level. Members of an ayllu had a duty, known as ayni, to help their fellows. This might be a collective task such as repairing or building a house, or assisting someone who was injured or had become ill until they were once again able to contribute to the overall weal.

The emperor's power was absolute, but his people had a right to expect a fair return for their work.

Between ayni and mit'a was the minka, a duty to assist with large-scale work benefiting several ayllu. Constructing and maintaining agricultural terraces or canals was beyond the capabilities of any one ayllu, but collectively the local community could accomplish a great deal without requiring assistance from the central authorities.

There does not seem to have been a merchant class in the Inca empire. Large-scale dealings were handled by government officials, and for the ordinary folk there was little need for merchants or shops. Good management ensured that little was wasted, and most transitions took the form of agreements to trade work for goods or bartering one item for another. A region suffering drought or a bad harvest could expect to have its needs met from the storehouses as soon as government officials heard of the problem.

This was the social contract upon which Inca society rested. The emperor's power was absolute, but his people had a right to expect a fair return for their work. They contributed labour that benefited the empire as a whole and sent food to be placed in the storehouses, knowing that when the time came that they needed something it would be provided. The system worked very well, without the need for a medium of currency, because it was built on strong social values. Had it broken down, Inca society might have descended into chaos. However, the Inca economy and the society it was built upon survived intact until dynastic war and the arrival of the Spanish jointly destroyed the empire.

## CONSOLIDATION AND EXPANSION

Having ensured the stability of his new empire, Pachacuti undertook great works in his capital at Cusco. Previous earth structures were rebuilt in stone, along with new palaces and temples. These were complemented by grand structures at other locations, consolidating the power of the new Inca empire. Since religion and political power were intertwined in Inca society, many of these structures are referred to as temple-fortresses. It is not always clear whether they were primarily a religious building with a good set of defences or a fort that contained a temple. In practice, the distinction may be meaningless; to the Inca they were the empire's strong places in both the mundane and the spiritual world.

BELOW: The Sacred Valley, north of Cusco, contains several major Inca archaeological sites. Among them is the Temple of the Moon, whose name was applied in modern times and may not reflect the site's original purpose.

These grand structures improved stability not only by providing a safe base for soldiers and leaders to operate from, but also by strengthening the religion of the local populace and reminding them of the emperor's power in this world and others. These measures worked; the Inca empire was strong and stable under Pachacuti.

Pachacuti died in 1471, plunging the empire into a year of mourning. Afterwards, a great celebration was observed and sacrifices were made. These included several hundred llamas and a large number of children, who were sacrificed at the places the emperor had visited. Pachacuti was mummified and his body occasionally displayed in public. It was found by the Spanish when they conquered the area and destroyed, though whether deliberately or otherwise is not known.

## INCA MUMMIES

The practice of mummification was used throughout the Andes, although not all burials involved it. Early cultures used alcohol and/or salt as preservatives, removing flesh and fluids to reduce decay. For the Incas, living at high altitudes with cold and dry conditions available, freeze-drying was a viable option. The mummy was then prepared for burial by being wrapped in cloth and tied into a foetal position with cords.

A different process of mummification was used for rulers and high nobles. The removal of organs and treatment of skin was intended to keep them as lifelike as possible. The mummified remains of these influential people were brought out of their burial places from time to time, to be consulted on state matters and to take part in rituals. They were ritually fed at these times. The mummies of children sacrificed in holy places high in the mountains were also brought offerings of food and drink. These sacrifices acted as intermediaries between humans and the gods, and could help ensure a fruitful growing season and a good harvest.

Rich grave-goods were provided to the mummies of important people, who were considered to retain ownership of property they had possessed in life. This made tombs attractive to

OPPOSITE: **A mummy from the Chauchilla Cemetery, a Nazca burial ground dating from before 900 AD. The extremely dry conditions there have resulted in some mummies retaining hair and skin for over a thousand years.**

# MACHU PICCHU

PERHAPS THE GREATEST WORK undertaken at the behest of Pachacuti was Machu Picchu, whose name means 'old hill'. This was another fortified temple, although it may be that the defences were intended mostly to limit access for ordinary people rather than to defeat a major enemy.

Machu Picchu was surrounded by a small town, which supported the priests who lived there. The nearby terrain was terraced to permit agriculture and prevent excessive water loss, permitting the site to be largely self-sufficient. Machu Picchu escaped destruction at the hands of Spanish

conquistadors largely because it had
fallen out of use by the time they arrived.
Although the local population knew of it,
they did not draw attention to its existence.
This enabled the site to survive, but its
significance has been lost to history. It
appears that the site aligns with a number

ABOVE: The Inca were conscious of how places
intersected on a spiritual level, and may have chosen
Machu Picchu for its alignment to other holy places.

of landmarks and human-made sites of
religious significance to the Inca, suggesting
it was an important ritual site.

opportunistic robbers and the systematic plundering of Spanish explorers. Once the Inca learned their royal grave sites were being targeted, they began moving the mummies of their former leaders to avoid detection. Ultimately, most were found.

## THE EMPIRE OF THE INCAS

The ruler of the empire was named Sapa Inca, meaning 'sole emperor', and today the empire is known after its ruler's title. Among its people, the empire was named Tawantinsuyu, meaning 'land of four quarters'.

The northernmost suyu, or quarter, was Chinchaysuyu, which extended up the coast of what is now Peru through Ecuador and into Colombia. The province was connected to the capital at Cusco by a great road named Qhapaq Nan, from which smaller routes radiated. The great road had storehouses

BELOW: The site at Sillustani was a burial ground for the Colla people, who were one of the early Inca conquests. The Inca allied with the enemies of the Colla, the Lupaca, and benefited from their allies' victory without taking part in the fighting.

and wayposts at intervals, and was in constant use by runners bearing messages to and from the capital.

The most southerly, and largest, of the quarters was Collasuyu, named for the Colla culture that existed on the shores of Lake Titicaca. Collasuyu contained numerous important holy sites as well as the Lake Titicaca region that was the centre of many myths.

To the southwest of Cusco lay Cuntisuyu. The terrain there was lower and dryer, and buildings tended to use adobe bricks rather than stone as in the highlands.

> The ruler of the empire was named Sapa Inca, meaning 'sole emperor', and today the empire is know after its ruler's title.

To the northeast of Cusco lay Antisuyu, named for its indigenous people. Western explorers later named the mountain chain Andes for the Anti people who lived there. Antisuyu was the least developed of the four quarters, and the Inca made little attempt to push eastwards beyond the fringes of the Amazonian rainforest. They did obtain wood and decorative materials such as feathers of exotic birds from the forest, but were not willing to challenge the local tribes by pushing too deeply into their territory.

From his capital at Cusco, the Sole Emperor ruled over a domain stretching from what is now Chile to Colombia, and from the Pacific coast to the Amazonian rainforest. He kept the provisional rulers close at hand at his capital in Cusco, ensuring their loyalty or at least reducing their ability to conduct a successful revolt.

Pachacuti is designated the ninth Sapa Inca, although he was the first to rule an empire from Cusco. His power was absolute, although he had assistance from a council of nobles and close family. Since the emperor claimed descent from the gods, his commands had religious significance and any action against him could be construed as an affront to the gods.

Governors of the Suyus were drawn from the high nobility and were supported by a large bureaucratic apparatus. They had power in most matters of law, except crimes for which the penalty was very severe. The laws they enforced were based on the traditional values of their people, and were aimed at creating a harmonious and productive society by promoting truthfulness, honesty and hard work.

Punishments were harsh, and were intended to deter others from breaking society's rules. However, for some minor crimes an official might do no more than administer a public reprimand that served as fair warning if the offence was repeated. Mutilation was common in the case of theft and antisocial behaviour, with the victim left alive to warn others against such behaviour. Mutilated offenders were reduced to begging for food in return for a graphic account of their punishment.

More serious crimes such as revolt, sedition, adultery and repeat offences after a reprimand had been given were punished by death in a variety of unpleasant ways. Stoning and hanging were

common, while some offenders were pushed from a high place to fall to their death. Executions were public as they were intended as a warning. At times, punishment could be collective, with a mass execution serving as a warning to those who witnessed it.

Although harsh, the Inca justice system followed values that had been ingrained into citizens since birth. Those who broke the law also went against the rules that enabled everyone to prosper and might well be seen as enemies of the people. Whether or not the general populace supported the rule of law, it worked well enough that there was little crime. This in turn contributed to stability and prosperity that benefited the common citizens of the empire as well as its rulers.

The expansion of the empire was conducted in a highly efficient fashion, consolidating gains before pushing outwards

LEFT: **An Inca army marching home from a successful campaign. Pack llamas transport booty and supplies, whilst captives are closely guarded. The Inca himself is carried by his attendants, surrounded by the elite of the army.**

again. The process began with emissaries, accompanied by a show of military strength. The empire offered the people of a new region the chance to join voluntarily, and would give lavish gifts to the existing rulers if they accepted Inca authority.

A governor would be appointed for the new territory. This would be a member of the emperor's family who therefore had a vested interest in maintaining the stability of the empire. The current elite were given new tasks, possibly in a distant area, but retained high status. Over time they were incorporated into the empire by marriage. This policy of making use of talented people experienced in leadership benefited the empire while ensuring they were not in a position to lead dissent among their own people.

Moving officials around the empire also meant that they had little in common with the people they governed in the new area, and were reliant on the empire rather than popular support to maintain their position. This policy has been successfully used by various empires throughout history, including the Romans, who would move troops from a conquered area to another part of the empire where they had no interest in the locals' causes for disaffection. The newly joined region lost its traditional rulers, who were replaced with others who had no interest in leading a rebellion, while the displaced elite left behind family members who could serve as hostages for their good behaviour.

Those who declined to join the empire were conquered. The Inca had an efficient military system and could rapidly bring to bear much greater force than any regional power. They could also supply that force for an extended period, so a campaign that went slower than expected would not result in having to withdraw when supplies ran out. The leaders of

BELOW: Tupac Amaru, depicted here blinding a captured enemy, briefly ruled a remnant of the Inca empire which remained outside Spanish control. With his capture and execution the Spanish destroyed any hope of a renewed Inca empire.

any resistance were executed in a manner guaranteed to intimidate any others who considered fighting for their independence.

## SUCCESSION AND CIVIL WAR

The emperor could have as many wives as he pleased, although his first wife was of paramount importance. Known as the Coya, she was a sister or half-sister of the Inca and was married to him the day he succeeded to the position. Only children of the Inca and Coya could inherit the title of emperor; those produced by his other wives could aspire to high station but would not rule. Age was not a factor in establishing primacy; instead the emperor chose whichever of his children with the Coya he believed to be most suitable. Some emperors named their heir as co-ruler later in life, enabling the emperor-to-be to receive on-the-throne instruction on how best to run the empire.

This may have been a reaction to the earlier situation in which the 'most skilful' of the ruler's children would inherit his position. Opinions naturally varied as to which of the children was most skilful and thus would inherit, resulting in assassinations, dubious alliances and the occasional civil war. The system used by Pachacuti and his descendants provided a clear line of succession and avoided the chaos that had traditionally accompanied the death of the Inca.

ABOVE: **Tupac Yupanqui led the armies of his father, Pachacuti, on a successful campaign into the north, defeating the Chimu people and extending the empire. He was chosen to succeed his father as Sapa Inca around 1471** AD.

Pachacuti chose his son Amaru Yupanqui to be his heir and co-ruler. Amaru seemed at first highly suitable; he was a good administrator and an expert on food production. In peaceful times, he would have been an excellent emperor. But these were not peaceful times, and despite Amaru's proven capabilities his father went against the established custom that once designated, the heir was destined to become emperor even if he proved unsuitable. He dismissed Amaru as heir and appointed his more warlike brother Tupac Yupanqui instead.

Amaru retained high status and acted as an emissary much of the time, while his brother continued to expand the empire. Huayna Capac succeeded Tupac in 1493, but failed to follow the established practice for succession. This was partly due to the wave of epidemics sweeping across South America as a result of contact with Europeans. His death in 1529 led to civil war between his sons Huascar and Atahualpa. Before his death, Huayna Capac had named his youngest son Ninan as his successor, not knowing that Ninan was also dying – probably of smallpox like his father.

Huascar had the strongest claim to the throne, as Atahualpa's mother was not a member of the Inca royal family. However, he was by all accounts an ill-tempered and unwise leader. Upon becoming Inca, Huascar attempted to put his half-brother in his place and demanded submission. Atahualpa sent gifts, which Huascar rebuffed by executing some of the emissaries. His accusation that Atahualpa was in revolt against

ABOVE: **Huascar was the logical choice to succeed his father due to his pure bloodline. He also had control of the capital, but his brother Atahualpa commanded the loyalty of the army and had his own powerbase in the north of the empire.**

the throne resulted in it becoming true; Atahualpa began making war upon his half-brother.

Thus began the Inca Dynastic War, sometimes known as the War of Two Brothers. Huascar held Cusco and had the support of the central government, but Atahualpa was popular in the north, where his mother's family had been rulers of their own people. From 1529 to 1532, the war ravaged the Inca empire, until Atahualpa defeated Huascar. Huascar was later executed along with his family, apparently securing Atahualpa's position as Inca. His reign was short-lived, however, as Spanish forces arrived soon after and the destruction of the Inca empire began.

## INCA WARFARE

The Inca understood very well that diplomacy and military force go hand in hand as tools of policy. Diplomacy is often more effective when the military option is available, and victory is meaningless unless translated into lasting gain. Their military was very much a tool of statecraft, and in general was used more often as a broad hint to potential foes than actually seeing action. There were exceptions, of course, such as when the kingdom of Cusco was fighting for its survival at the beginning of the era, and during the civil war at the end.

The Inca military depended upon a similar system to the mit'a. Men aged between 20 and 50 could be called for military service on a rotating basis, and would be grouped into units based on their region of origin. The

BELOW: A depiction of Inca warriors, showing their highly decorated clothing and headdresses. The Inca system permitted a large force to be quickly raised, and combined with excellent logistics this enabled the empire to bring overwhelming numbers to any battle.

empire included numerous ethnic groups, many with their own language and customs, making the creation of a fully integrated force problematic. Units raised from ethnic Inca formed elite formations distinguished by their clothing, and often served as a reserve of bodyguard for the commander.

Units were in multiples of ten, creating formations of 10, 100, 1000 and 10,000 men each with its own leaders and commanders. It seems that officers were paired, although whether they had complementary duties much like a warship's captain and executive officer or they somehow shared command is not known.

Although this system permitted large numbers to be raised, it did not produce a particularly effective fighting force. The army was highly organized but incorporated a large number of non-combatants. These included baggage carriers and the wives of soldiers, and the warriors themselves were not trained professionals. Inca men were not entirely untutored in the arts of war, however. They would receive some instruction with common weapons in their youth, and might take part in ritualized combat from time to time.

### INCA WEAPONS AND TACTICS

The weapons used by a given unit depended on its ethnic origins. Light spears or darts projected with an atlatl were used for skirmishing, although bows and slings were preferred by some groups. For close combat, spears and clubs were popular, along with a sword-like weapon made from hardwood or a mace with a star-shaped head made of metal.

For protection, the Inca warrior had a light shield and body armour made from quilted cloth, possibly with small metal plates attached. He might also wear a feathered headdress and items commemorating previous successes such as trophies from slain enemies or jewellery gifted to him by a commander.

Leadership was not of the heroic sort. Rather than lead their men personally, Inca commanders remained behind the fighting line and directed the army. Strategically, the Inca relied on rapid movement and getting a large force into the field at the critical

OPPOSITE: **This painted scene depicts Inca warriors in combat. After the initial exchange of darts and javelins a battle would quickly degenerate into a close-quarters scramble in which the advantage lay with the more numerous and more aggressive side.**

point. It was their superior organization and logistics that gave them the advantage in most conflicts rather than any superiority in personal or army-level fighting power.

Inca tactics followed on from this, and were primarily based on overwhelming numbers applied with aggression and tenacity. Where possible, the enemy would be won over with generous

peace terms backed up by the threat of the army, and if this failed a period of almost ritualized confrontation allowed the enemy's resolve to be weakened with chanting, warlike shouts and threats. If this was not sufficient, then a period of skirmishing followed by a headlong charge was a common tactic, with battles descending into a confused scramble of small-scale personal combat.

This mode of warfare was effective against the smaller states encountered by the Incas in their expansion, but proved bloody and often indecisive in their civil war. Against the Spanish newcomers and their entirely different way of making war it failed completely.

## INCA RELIGION

Our understanding of the Inca religion is based on records made by Spanish chroniclers and tales that have survived centuries of outside influence. As with all meetings of very different cultures, the Spanish did not fully understand the Inca religion and in many cases were not concerned with its details. Having seen enough to denounce it as heresy, some of those who might have written a record set about destroying the Inca faith instead. Even those who genuinely wanted to learn had to overcome their own preconceptions and a natural tendency to equate Inca gods to concepts they already understood.

The Spanish set about converting the Inca and the surrounding peoples to Christianity, ensuring that traditional Inca beliefs and stories would become intermixed with Christian values over time. Records produced after contact with Europeans, even where they were made with genuine intentions to preserve the old religion, do not necessarily reflect the beliefs of the Incas before contact.

BELOW: **Along with darts and javelins, the sling was a common Inca weapon. Cheap and easy to make, it had the additional advantage that many men would have experience using a sling for hunting.**

The creator of the world, Viracocha, was almost an abstract concept whose name may have been forbidden to commoners. It has been suggested that the various surviving creation stories may reflect the versions told by people who were allowed to name Viracocha and those who were not. Viracocha created the world and everything in it, then departed over the Pacific Ocean. He left behind a pantheon of gods to watch over his people and to personify the many aspects of the natural world.

Foremost among the Inca gods was Inti, the sun god. The greatest of temples were built in his honour, decorated with gold in a manner intended to reflect the light and glory of the sun. Inti was the founder of the ruling dynasty; the emperor derived his semi-divine status from this descent and spoke with the authority of the gods themselves.

It is possible that worship of Inti was reserved for the upper echelons of society, although at least some the general populace were able to participate in the most important ritual of the year;

ABOVE: **Viracocha (left) was the creator-god, whose very name may have been forbidden to commoners. Viracocha's abstract nature meant that the sun god Inti (right) was a more accessible deity for most people.**

ABOVE: The Inti Raymi
Festival of the Sun is
still celebrated at Cusco,
albeit in a modified form
which does not include
blood sacrifice. The huge
spectacle culminates in an
oration by the Sapa Inca
and the re-enactment of
Inca rituals.

the Inti Raymi. This took place on the winter solstice, which
began on 21 June. The ceremony was intended to bring the sun
god back, and reached its peak on 24 June.

The Inti Raymi ceremony began with fasting and purification,
followed by feasting and merriment. Sacrifices were made
including llamas and – according to some chroniclers – children.
The ceremony was outlawed by the Spanish after they conquered
the Inca empire, but carried on in a diminished form and has
survived to this day.

As the Inca was associated with Inti the sun god, so his
wife the Coya was associated with Mama Quilla, goddess of
the moon. Mama Quilla was a protector of women, although
it seems she was not widely worshipped. Illapa was of great
importance to most ordinary people as the god of weather and
the bringer of rain. He also had some functions in connection

with warfare. Zaramamma was also highly significant throughout Inca society as the goddess of maize.

Supay, god of death and the underworld, was equated with the Christian devil by Spanish chroniclers, but was in reality quite different. Supay was associated with Mama Pacha, the earth goddess, and was a figure to be feared and propitiated. However, he was also worshipped by miners, who hoped he would spare them from the dangers of working underground while rewarding their labours. After the Spanish conquest, many Inca people were forced to work in mines, strengthening the connection between Supay of the Inca underworld and the Christian devil. He is still revered today among South American miners and underground workers.

## SAPA INCA

The Incas had many other gods, some of them worshipped by groups they brought into their empire. So long as the conquered or absorbed people accepted Itzi as the supreme god and the Sapa Inca as his representative, they were permitted to retain their own religion. This acceptance of foreign gods was easier for a polytheistic empire like the Incas, compared to a monotheistic society such as the Spanish. It was also a wise political move – in many cases, people will remain content or at least docile upon finding they are paying taxes to a different master, but can be moved to great violence if deprived of their gods.

The Sapa Inca had a religious function as well as a political one, and could be considered a priest-king, but there was also an organized religious class that trained young priests under more experienced ones and staffed the great temples. The supreme authority among the priesthood held the title Villac Umu and was almost as powerful as the emperor. He appointed and could dismiss priests, and was responsible for all temples and shrines throughout the empire.

BELOW: Mama Pacha was a goddess of the earth and of fertility, whose favour ensured good crops. A libation of chicha de jora (corn beer) would be poured on the ground in her honour before the rest was drunk.

In addition to the human-made holy places, the priesthood made use of places said to have oracular powers, and conduced divinations using smoke, herbs or the lungs of a sacrificed llama. Psychotropic substances were used to assist in communing with the other world, notably ayahuasca, a drink made from a combination of plant extracts.

The religion of the Incas was inextricably intertwined with their social and cultural values and even economic activity. Thus, when the Spanish arrived and began forcibly converting the Inca people they destroyed the very fabric of society.

## ARRIVAL OF THE SPANISH

The first European expeditions to arrive in the 'New World' landed on islands in the Caribbean, and represented something of a failure in terms of the original intent. The purpose of these expeditions was to find a way to the East Indies, but it soon became apparent that there was money to be made in this newly discovered region. The dual Spanish monarchy of Ferdinand of Aragon and Isabella of Castile initially stated that the local

BELOW: Ayahuasca was a psychotropic drink used for spiritual purposes by the Inca. It is still taken today, though its use is controversial and has in some cases become part of a 'modern mysticism' culture which has little to do with Inca religion.

population were to be treated with kindness and treated fairly, but the lure of riches was too great and the exploration of the New World took on the aspect of a treasure hunt.

As the powers of Europe scrambled to take advantage of the newly discovered opportunities, exploration missions landed on the northern and southern American continents and pushed inland. Many were ill planned, badly supplied and led by opportunists with little idea of what they were doing. Others, despite competent leadership and lavish support, met an unfortunate fate. The expedition led by Francisco Pizarro had distinctly mixed fortunes at first but ultimately brought down the Inca empire – largely due to a stroke of luck regarding the timing of their arrival.

ABOVE: Francisco Pizarro's conquest of the Inca empire was due to a combination of opportunism and desperation. Placed in a perilous situation he staked everything on a single attack taking advantage of European weaponry.

Initial contact with Europeans had caused a series of epidemics, notably smallpox, among the people of South America. In addition to weakening the Inca empire by killing off large numbers of workers upon whom the economy depended, disease also caused the untimely death of the Sapa Inca Huayna Capac, and his young heir. His sons Huascar and Atahualpa fought a bloody civil war for possession of the empire.

Huascar advanced against Atahualpa's position in the north but was defeated at Riobamba. Atahualpa then drove south into the lands of the Cañari people near Tumi Pampas. The Cañari offered little assistance to Huascar, attempting to stay out of the conflict, but nevertheless Atahualpa was defeated and captured. After making his escape, Atahualpa ravaged the lands of the Cañari in a possibly misplaced act of vengeance and won a series of victories over his enemy, culminating in the defeat and capture of Huascar at Cusco.

Atahualpa was at this time aware of a small band of foreigners causing trouble in what was now his empire. Pizarro's expedition, numbering around 160 men, was in communication with both factions and offered to assist Atahualpa against Huascar. Atahualpa was at Cajamarca at the time, celebrating his victory, when the Spaniards arrived.

Suspicion between Atahualpa and Pizarro – and their followers – was deep. The Spaniards numbered only a few dozen, though they had horses, light artillery and firearms, while Atahualpa had around 7000 warriors with him.

**Pizarro correctly presumed that if he could capture Atahualpa he would gain control of the Inca empire.**

Pizarro knew his tiny force was isolated with no hope of rescue or assistance, and he was sure Atahualpa intended to attack. Yet the two exchanged apparently friendly messages, inviting one another to visit in guaranteed safety. They promised to greet one another as brothers and swear friendship.

The Spaniards passed a fearful night in Cajamarca in which few members of the expedition got any sleep. Pizarro decided that his only chance was to strike hard and fast, so concealed his horsemen ready to charge and set up arquebusiers and cannon ready in position to fire as soon as he commanded it. For his part, Atahualpa was overconfident. His men ostentatiously set aside their weapons and he personally went to meet the Spaniards with only a small guard of honour.

Pizarro's expedition offered Atahualpa a proposal that must have seemed ludicrous at the time. The Sapa Inca – sole emperor and descendant of the gods – would be permitted to keep his throne if he submitted to the authority of Spain and accept Christianity as his faith. This was unthinkable, as it meant casting aside all that the Sapa Inca was.

Unsurprisingly, negotiations broke down. It is not clear who initiated violence but once it started the fight was savage. The Inca had never faced firearms or artillery before, and were introduced to their capabilities with a short-range fusillade. This was followed by a cavalry charge, which was also beyond their experience.

Pizarro correctly presumed that if he could capture Atahualpa he would gain control of the Inca empire. The Sapa Inca was on a litter supported by his unarmed attendants, who tried to stop the Spanish charge by acting as a human wall. Others did their best to support the litter with the stumps of severed limbs, but soon Atahualpa was taken prisoner. The Spanish chased down his fleeing guards and killed everyone they caught.

## DESTRUCTION OF THE EMPIRE

The Sapa Inca was permitted to rule his empire from captivity in Cajamarca, receiving visits from officials who assured him that his orders to execute Huascar had been carried out. A ransom was agreed between Atahualpa and Pizarro; a large room was

ABOVE: Atahualpa expected that the foreigners would be awed into submission by the majesty of the Sapa Inca and his warriors. It might have worked with a different opponent, but Pizarro's men were convinced that violence was their only option.

ABOVE: Atahualpa's captors ensured they wrung as much as possible out of the deal for his release by flattening vessels and smashing gold sculptures. This made them take up less room, requiring even more gold to fill the designated space.

selected and Atahualpa told his captor that it would be filled half full with gold to secure his release. Four times that amount of silver was also promised. The Inca empire proved quite capable of delivering this enormous quantity of precious metals, although it was necessary to remove gold from temples and to gather silver from every available source.

The Spanish were still very aware that they were in a foreign city far from any possible assistance, and their immense haul of gold would be of no value if Atahualpa's armies fell on them after his release. The Sapa Inca seems to have genuinely believed that he would be freed, as he gave instructions not to attempt a rescue. Despite this, rumours reached Cajamarca that an army was on its way. The fearful Spaniards accused Atahualpa of treachery and Pizarro ordered that he be burned at the stake.

Although he had resisted pressure to convert while in captivity,

Atahualpa now faced a stark choice. If he remained true to his beliefs he would be burned. He was offered the slightly less grim alternative of execution by garrotting, but only if he took the Catholic faith. He was put to death in July 1533, after which the Spanish installed his brother Tupac Huallca as emperor.

## INCAS UNDER SPANISH RULE

A series of Spanish-controlled puppet rulers came to an end with the death of Tupac Amarru in 1572, by which time the former empire of the Incas was firmly under Spanish rule. In addition to plundering temples of every scrap of gold that could be removed and destroying the mummies of previous notables, the Spanish forced their religion upon their new subject people. This broke down an essential part of the Inca way of life, which had already been dealt a mortal blow by the end of the divine line of Incas.

The Spanish made use of some vestiges of Inca culture. The concept of the mit'a was used to force people to work in the mines, extracting precious metals for their new overlords. In theory, the workers would be permitted to go home once their obligation had been paid off, but the system was set up so that the workers got further into debt to their masters instead. As a result, not only did most workers never return from the mines, but family members were sometimes rounded up and brought in to replace those who had died.

The Spanish conquerors justified their actions towards Atahualpa by claiming he was a usurper and that they had intervened in an effort to restore the rightful emperor. Atahualpa was vilified in official histories and made a scapegoat for the destruction of an entire civilization in the name of greed and opportunism.

BELOW: It will never be known if Atahualpa would have let the Spanish leave with their gold. Rumours of a rescue attempt prompted Pizarro to order his execution, after which they installed their own puppet ruler.

CHAPTER 5

# The Aztec Civilization

The Aztec empire was the last of the great Mesoamerican civilizations. It was created by warfare and conquest, and fell the same way. In its heyday, the empire had 15 million citizens across most of northern Mesoamerica.

THE AZTEC EMPIRE was the only Mesoamerican civilization to be directly contacted by Europeans at its height. Remnants of the Maya were encountered – and conquered – by the Spanish, but by this time their civilization was in deep decline. The Aztecs, on the other hand, were a powerful and mature culture with strong central leadership.

Much of what is known about the earlier Mesoamerican civilizations was learned from the Aztecs, who may or may not have fully understood the culture of their predecessors. Hundreds of years had passed from the fall of the Olmec civilization to the founding of the Aztec empire. Although histories had been passed down in the form of oral traditions and cultural practices derived from those of earlier societies, distortion was inevitable even with the best of intentions. The Aztecs particularly admired the Toltec civilization, which they saw as a model society. They plundered

OPPOSITE: The conquest of the Aztec empire was not straightforward. Spanish forces were driven from Tenochtitlán on 30 June 1520, in an event known to the Spanish as *La Noche Triste*, or The Night of Sadness.

OPPOSITE: Aztec boys were taught essential skills such as using a canoe, and if they failed to meet their father's standards the punishments were harsh.

BELOW: The Aztecs admired the Toltec civilization, and plundered many of its treasures. Artefacts like this incense holder are common finds in Aztec sites.

the declining cities of the Toltecs, not so much for wealth as for cultural treasures. The nobility of the Aztec empire claimed descent from the Toltecs, and naturally presented their supposed ancestors in as positive a light as possible. Thus, much of what was learned from early Spanish chroniclers about the Toltecs was of questionable veracity.

As for the Aztecs themselves, the observations of these first chroniclers were made amid a clash of cultures. The Spanish had arrived in a strange land with very different customs to any civilization in Europe, and in many cases failed to comprehend what they were witnessing. They also looked upon the Aztec empire with a mindset coloured by religious bigotry and a desire to plunder the riches of the New World.

Later investigation by way of archaeology and investigation of oral histories retained by the people of the former Aztec empire has provided a clearer picture of their way of life. Details are still emerging, and many long-believed myths refuse to be dispelled. Despite this, the Aztec civilization is the best understood of the indigenous Mesoamerican cultures.

## THE VALLEY OF MEXICO

The Valley of Mexico is a highland plateau over 2200m (7220ft) above sea level, surrounded by mountains. In the past it contained several large lakes, although modern drainage and water use have greatly lowered the water table in the region. With plenty of water and a mild climate, the valley was ideal for human habitation, which began at least 12,000 years ago. Abundant food production allowed complex cultures to arise, including those of Teotihuacán, the Toltec civilization and later the Aztec empire.

The modern name for the region – and the country surrounding it – comes from Mexica, one of the peoples who inhabited the area. The Mexica were not native to the region, but probably migrated south from what is now the southwestern USA. Their point of origin and the date

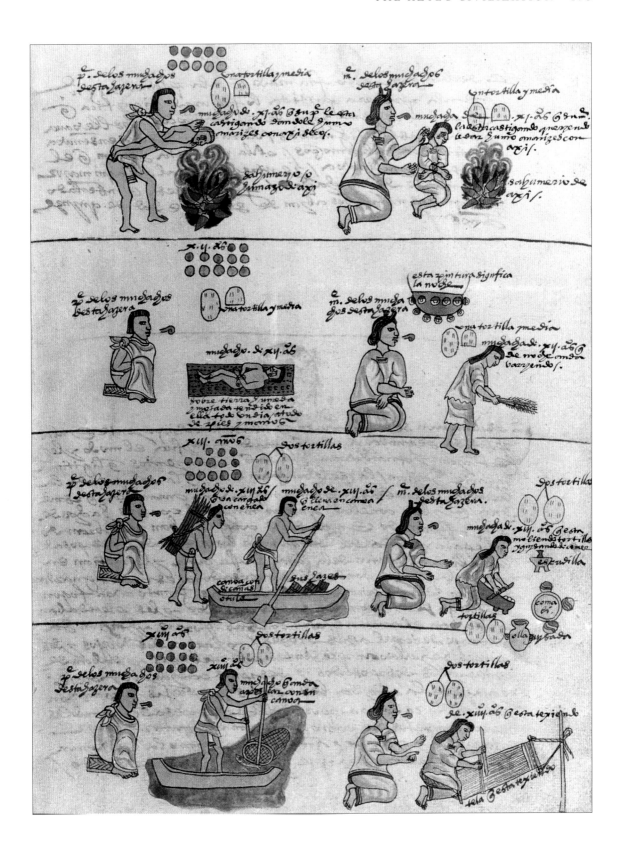

BELOW: A post-conquest
codex depicting the daily
life of the Aztec people.
All such sources are of
course filtered through
the preconceptions of
the creator, and may not
reflect the situation before
the arrival of the Spanish.

of their entry into Mesoamerica are both open to debate. It is possible that the ancestors of the Aztecs arrived in the Valley of Mexico as early as 1100 AD, although a later date is more probable. They are believed to have lived a nomadic or semi-nomadic lifestyle, wandering the valley for several decades before groups began to settle down permanently. One such settlement was at Lake Texcoco around 1248 AD.

Lake Texcoco was formed during the Ice Age, and was originally very extensive. As the climate warmed it was fed with

meltwater for many centuries and underwent several periods of expansion. However, the overall trend was towards drainage and a lowering of the water level. Eventually what remained was a group of lakes that were at times connected to Lake Texcoco depending on recent climate conditions.

There is evidence of human habitation around the lake for 7000 years or so. Its fluctuations caused settlements to be relocated and destroyed some of the archaeological evidence that might have given a clearer insight into the culture of these people, but eventually complex societies began to appear. Notable among these was Teotihuacán, which flourished until around 500 AD and lingered on in a greatly diminished form until 700–800 AD.

By 1100 AD, the Valley of Mexico was home to numerous city-states, termed altepetl. These small states vied with one another for political and economic advantage, and sometimes came into direct conflict. The arrival of migratory people added complexity to the political situation, and may have directly or indirectly contributed to the fall of some of these powers.

ABOVE: It is probable, though not certain, that the city of Tula which lay about 70km (43 miles) from Tenochtitlán, was the semi-mythical 'Tollan', capital of the Toltec civilization. The city was extensively plundered by the Aztec empire, seeking art and cultural objects.

RIGHT: A stone carving of a warrior from the Toltec civilization, found at Tula. Dating stone artefacts typically relies on identifying a style, as radiocarbon dating requires the presence of biological matter.

According to the Aztecs, the greatest and most civilized power in the region when they arrived was the Toltec culture, centred on its capital at Tollan. The Aztecs represent the Toltecs as advanced in technology and culture, wise and learned. Their skills enabled them to produce excellent goods that they traded for riches, while their fields overflowed with maize. There is archaeological evidence to back up some of these claims, and certainly the Toltec civilization would have been impressive enough to awe a group of semi-nomadic hunter-gatherers.

The Toltecs were warlike, and had survived numerous conflicts during their history. However, this did not prevent the rapid decline of their society. Tollan was sacked around 1150 AD, at a time roughly corresponding to the arrival of the Aztecs' ancestors. It is probable that the Toltecs suffered an internal conflict that rendered them unable to resist external pressures. A segment of the Toltec people

## ALTEPETL AND EMPIRE

THE WORD ALTEPETL COMES from 'water' and 'hill', implying a suitable living place. It came to mean a small state with central authority, comprising a single city and its surrounding towns and villages. The power of these city-states varied; some commanded tribute from several other cities, while others were kept from flourishing by the same tribute requirements. The altepetl system was not replaced after the rise of the Aztec empire. Instead, the most powerful of the city-states came to command direct tribute from a number of smaller states, and from the tributary cities of their more powerful vassal states. The Aztec empire was a pyramid of tributary responsibilities rather than a unified state.

moved to Chapultepec on the shores of Lake Texcoco around 1150–1170, where they remained influential in local affairs.

Other cities became increasingly important during this period. The region around the former Toltec cities of Azcapotzalco and Tepanec was claimed by a group related to the ancestors of the Aztecs. It is not clear whether the emerging state became known by the name of one of its cities, or whether the tribe was called Tepanec and the city was renamed after them. The city of Tetzcoco was founded by the Acolhua, another group with common origins to the Aztecs. The Tepanecs and Acolhua would come to be the major powers of the Valley of Mexico before the upheavals that led to the creation of the Aztec empire.

## ORIGINS OF THE AZTECS

The Aztecs and their related cultures told tales of their place of origin, which they called Aztlán, or 'white land'. Its location is open to debate, but was probably somewhere in northern Mexico. Although known to history as the Aztecs after the (possibly mythical) land of Aztlán, the people who came to dominate the Valley of Mexico had other names for themselves. Their name for Lake Texcoco was Metzliapan ('moon lake'); the name Mexica for the people of the region probably came from this. From their legendary ancestor they took the name Tenocha. They also used the name Culhua-Mexica, which implied a connection with the greatly admired Toltecs.

The Aztecs and their related cultures spoke Nahuatl, part of the Uto-Aztecan language family. This reinforces the belief that their point of origin was well to the north of the Valley of Mexico; their language family included the tongues of the Hopi, Shoshone and many other

BELOW: Spanish missionaries learned Nahuatl, the Aztec language, in order to spread their beliefs. The Spanish-Nahuatl dictionary compiled by Alonso de Molina in the mid 1500s is still used by some scholars.

native North American tribes. It is probable that Nahuatl reached the Valley of Mexico around 400–500 AD, brought by small numbers of migrants from the north. Subsequent arrivals made the language more common. By the time of the Aztec empire, it was spoken sufficiently widely to act as a 'trade language' among the people of the region.

Nahuatl survived the conquest of Mesoamerica by the Spanish, and was adopted by the new overlords for much the same purpose as it had served the Aztecs. In addition to being used for trade and diplomacy, Spanish clergymen were taught Nahuatl in order to convey their religion to the people they hoped to convert. Although it has naturally evolved over time, Nahuatl is still spoken today.

The Valley of Mexico was an ideal location for the rise of a civilization. Agriculture using the chinampa method permitted

BELOW: Created in 1704 by Giovanni Francesco Gemelli Careri, the 'Gamelli map' depicts the migration of the proto-Aztec people from their mythical homeland of Aztlán to Chapultepec. It contains spiritual as well as physical elements.

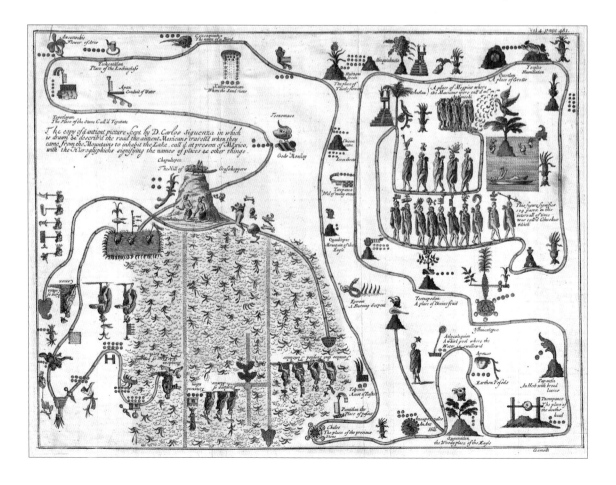

# CULTURAL INHERITANCE AND CULTURAL DRIFT

THE AZTEC CIVILIZATION HAD much in common with the Maya and other Mesoamerican cultures as a result of common ancestry. Hundreds of years had passed since the earliest Mesoamerican civilizations had arisen, and their ideas, values and gods had spread throughout the region. Thus there are similarities between some Aztec gods and those of the Toltecs or the Maya; in some cases, the same deities were worshipped. However, time and contact with new societies altered and distorted these beliefs, and even within the fairly short time frame of the Aztec empire the beliefs of its people changed.

It is the nature of belief that soon the new version of a legend is thought to be 'how it always was', so any recorded tale or depiction must be taken as a snapshot of what was believed at that time and place rather than being a universal truth applicable throughout the whole Aztec empire over its entire history.

support of a large society, and the ability to use water transport on the lakes of the valley offset the lack of wheels or animals capable of carrying or pulling heavy loads. Remnants of previous civilizations existed there when the Mexica arrived, along with the states of groups who had migrated south earlier than the Mexica.

The Mexica attempted to settle at Chapultepec, a less than ideal location but one that was not claimed by better-established groups. The nearby city of Culhuacan demanded tribute from them and essentially became their overlords for a time, but after Mexica warriors provided valuable assistance to Culhuacan they were sent a daughter of its ruler to serve as a priestess. Unfortunately, the gods of the Mexica demanded she be sacrificed, which soured relations with Culhuacan.

Driven from their new home by Culhuacan, the Mexica moved on until they found a suitable spot on an island in Lake Texcoco. There the city of Tenochtitlán was founded, according to tradition, in 1325 or 1345. Tenochtitlán was at the time one of many altepetls in the region, and was initially of little importance.

# THE FOUNDING OF TENOCHTITLÁN

ABOVE: According to legend, the site of Tenochtitlán was chosen using the power of the heart taken from a powerful defeated enemy. This revealed a final sign from the gods that the Aztecs had found their new home.

ACCORDING TO AZTEC LEGEND, the ancestors of the Aztecs were guided in their migration from Aztlán into what is now Mexico by an idol of the god Huitzilopochtli. The idol promised the Aztecs prosperity if they followed its directions, which were apparently less than clear. The Aztecs repeatedly settled down, only to have to move on when their chosen site turned out to be unsuitable. Eventually, some of them tired of the march and conflict broke out. The rebels were led by Copil, whose mother was the goddess Malinalxochitl. Sister to Huitzilopochtli, Malinalxochitl resented not being worshipped and wished to lead the Aztecs astray. Fighting took place between the followers of the two gods, with Copil eventually being defeated. Huitzilopochtli directed that Copil's heart be flung into Lake Texcoco; where it landed would be the new home of his people. They did as required and saw an eagle eating a snake while perched on a prickly-pear cactus, a sign from the gods that they were in the right place. So the capital of what would become the Aztec empire was founded.

The two main threats faced by the city-state of Tenochtitlán were the Acolhua, with their capital at Texcoco, and the Tepanec, whose capital was at Azcapotzalco. According to legend, the Aztecs were the least advanced and most uncivilized of the people of the region when they arrived. However, they wanted to learn better ways and in particular studied the fallen Toltecs. From them, the Aztecs learned the secrets of becoming a great power.

## TENOCHTITLÁN

Having founded their new city, the Aztecs needed to integrate themselves into the local political landscape, which meant at the very least gaining sufficient power to avoid becoming victims of their warlike neighbours. Tenochtitlán itself was highly defensible due to its island location, but having to cross the lake in order to go anywhere would have made conducting trade or projecting power a difficult business. Three causeways were built, connecting the city and the shore to the east, west and north, with gaps crossed by removable bridges. The city was never directly attacked before the arrival of the Spanish, but if it had been the bridges were intended to deny an enemy easy access while allowing the defenders to come out to fight at will.

> According to legend, the Aztecs were the least advanced and most uncivilized of the people of the region when they arrived.

The central district was, as in many Mesoamerican cities, dedicated to religion. In addition to the temples of many gods, the central area had a ceremonial ball court, all dominated by temples of Tlaloc and Huitzilopochtli. These stood atop a pyramid named Hueteocalli, otherwise known as the Great Temple or Temple Mayor.

Hueteocalli stood at the centre of the Aztec capital and also, politically and spiritually, at the centre of the Aztec empire. The temple to Tlaloc, god of rain, stood on the north side of the pyramid and was aligned with the summer solstice. The temple of Huitzilopochtli, god of war, was aligned with the winter solstice on the south side of the pyramid. At the base of the pyramid steps a stone monument commemorated the goddess

Coyolxauhqui, who was slain by Huitzilopochtli and hurled down a mountainside; the corpses of human sacrifices were flung down the pyramid steps in a similar manner after their hearts had been cut out.

The remainder of Tenochtitlán was built on a grid pattern, with four quarters divided by the main roads through the city. With no animal-drawn vehicles to accommodate, streets did not have to be wide and most movement was on foot. Water transport was also used, with boats carrying goods along the city's canals. This allowed food to be brought directly into the city from the chinampas built in the surrounding lake. Chinampa-based agriculture was used out of necessity, since there was little useable land around the lake, but had the additional effect of making it difficult for an enemy to cut off the city's

BELOW: **A reconstructed map of Tenochtitlán, showing the main thoroughfares, temples and canals. The city's defences were augmented by removable bridges over sections of the causeways, though these were eventually circumvented by Spanish ships operating on the lake.**

food supply without gaining control of the waters.

## RISE OF THE TRIPLE ALLIANCE

As the people of Tenochtitlán built their home city, they gained in power through trade with their neighbours. Some cities could be reached by boat using the waterways around Lake Texcoco; others by overland trading parties. By 1350, the Valley of Mexico was divided among the territories of numerous tlatoani, or petty-kings. Each ruled an altepetl, or city-state, which controlled a modest amount of nearby territory.

ABOVE: The canals of Tenochtitlán enabled people and goods to be moved around in relative ease. In a society without beasts of burden or wheeled conveyances, water transport was a cheap and effective alternative.

Initially, no altepetl was dominant. Shifting alliances ensured that no one city-state could emerge as pre-eminent, but over time this began to change. Against a backdrop of intermittent conflict between city-states, two powers began to emerge. Tepaneca dominated the western side of the valley; Acolhua the east. The increasing power of Tepaneca enabled the city to bring more of the valley under its control and to impose heavy tribute demands.

Around 1416–18, Texcoco was defeated by the Tepaneca with the support of Tenochtitlán, which received the city as a tributary state. The prince of Texcoco, Nezahualcoyotl, was maintained in high status at Tenochtitlán and apparently became friendly towards his captors. Meanwhile, relations between Tenochtitlán and the Tepaneca became strained, eventually leading to open conflict.

Tenochtitlán was allied with Acolhua at the time, and together they were able to defeat the forces of the Tepaneca. Nezahualcoyotl reclaimed the throne of Texcoco, and remained

ABOVE: The city of Tlatelolco remained independent of Tenochtitlán long after more distant cities had been conquered. It was the commercial capital of the Aztec world, and came to be seen as a potential threat to the empire.

OPPOSITE: Nezahualcoyotl was the king-in-exile of Texcoco, given refuge by the leaders of Tenochtitlán. He was a steadfast ally in their war against the Tepanec emperor, which ultimately lead to the formation of the Aztec empire.

favourably inclined towards Tenochtitlán. Their victories inspired the city-state of Tlacopan to desert the Tepaneca cause and enter into a Triple Alliance with Tenochtitlán and the restored Acolhua capital of Texcoco. Formalized in 1428, this alliance was the foundation of the Aztec empire.

After defeating the Tepaneca and capturing their capital at Azcapotzalco, the Triple Alliance extended its dominion over the Valley of Mexico. A campaign in the south was successfully concluded in 1432, with most of the valley subjugated by 1460. Despite being located very close to Tenochtitlán, Tlatelolco was not conquered until 1473. Tlatelolco was, according to legend, founded in 1337 by a breakaway group from Tenochtitlán. The city became a major trading centre, wielding enormous economic power. This eventually prompted the Aztec emperor Axayacatl to annex Tlatelolco in order to end any potential threat.

The Triple Alliance was highly successful but did not create a fully integrated empire in the European sense. Each of the three member cities controlled a number of other altepetl as tributary states, and was an autonomous polity. Thus, the Triple Alliance controlled an empire, rather than it being ruled by a single city. Each member received a proportion of the booty from conquest – 40% to each of Tenochtitlán and Texcoco and 20% to Tlacopan – after which its ruler was free to do as he pleased with the money.

Tenochtitlán emerged as the primary military centre of the Triple Alliance, and Texcoco as a centre for learning. For many years, the empire was stable despite its internal divisions. However, there was never any real movement towards true political unity and at times the member city-states were at

Collection E. Eug. GOUPIL à Paris
Nᵒ 65271.
Ancienne Collection J. M. A. AUBIN

odds with one another. The overall goals of the empire were maintained, but internal politics could be complex.

The ruling elite of the three Alliance cities and their most important subordinate states shared a vested interest in maintaining control of the whole valley and ensuring that all of their tributary states prospered. At the same time, each was aware that the others were potential rivals or even enemies who could not be allowed to grow too powerful. Tenochtitlán attempted to increase its political control over the other alliance members by influencing dynastic marriages and eroding the status of its rivals. It was successful in regard to Tlacopan; less so with Texcoco.

> Tenochtitlán attempted to increase its political control over the other alliance members by influencing dynastic marriages.

Eventually, Tenochtitlán came to be the more-or-less dominant power in an empire ruled by an alliance of city-states. Stability permitted prosperity, and prosperity translated to power. The Aztec empire reached its height just as the first Europeans were arriving in the New World.

### KINGS OF TENOCHTITLÁN

According to legend, the first ruler of Tenochtitlán was Tenoch, who may or may not have been a real person. Tenoch is something of a 'legendary ancestor figure' who may have been based on one or more real leaders, or could have been a real person about whom stories and myths later sprang up. Tenoch is credited with leading the Mexica people to their home at Tenochtitlán, dying in 1375 after establishing the city. His successor was Acamapichtli, who claimed descent from the noble houses of the Toltecs as well as the Mexica.

Acamapichtli's father was a warrior of the Mexica people; his mother a noblewoman from Culhuacan. Culhuacan was a remnant of the Toltec civilization and – according to legend – still a glorious seat of learning and culture. Acamapichtli benefited from a good start in life and was highly accomplished, although still young, when he was asked to become ruler of Tenochtitlán.

Tenochtitlán was at the time a large town of no great importance, and it was Acamapichtli who oversaw its early expansion and the development of its trade network. He was friendly to the Acolhua people of nearby cities, among whom he spent much of his early life, and was able to build on these relationships over time. However, Tenochtitlán was under the domination of the Tepaneca, who demanded high tribute and initially allowed Acamapichtli to serve only as a governor rather than a ruler in his own right.

Tenochtitlán supplied warriors to fight in the campaigns of the Tepanec overlords, and paid its tribute diligently. This seems to have been a wise policy; after 1383, Acamapichtli is depicted differently in surviving glyphs, suggesting that he had been named tlatoani – the word translates directly as 'speaker' but can be taken as meaning king, or ruler – of Tenochtitlán.

Acamapichtli benefited from his association with the Toltecs. Blood relationships and membership of a noble line were highly regarded, giving Acamapichtli advantages in negotiations with

BELOW: The Codex Mendoza was probably commissioned by Don Antonio de Mendoza, soon after the conquest of the Aztec empire. It contained a history of their leaders – including Tenoch, seen here – and their deeds.

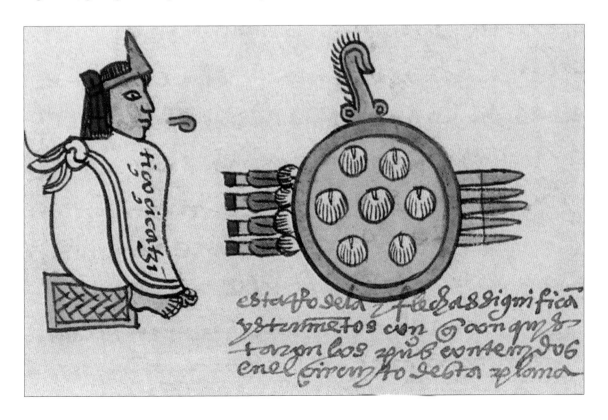

BELOW: **Acamapichtli (top) laid the foundations of the Aztec empire by expanding the economic base of Tenochtitlán. Chimalpopoca (bottom) enhanced the city's status and reduced its tribute requirements**

other city-states. He took numerous wives, one from each district within Tenochtitlán in addition to his first who was from Culhuacan. Tenochtitlán was still very much a subordinate of the Tepaneca, but under Acamapichtli it grew in importance and trust. The city's agricultural base was greatly expanded during his reign, and he was eventually permitted to lead military expeditions without direct oversight from Azcapotzalco, the Tepanec capital. Before his death in 1391, Acamapichtli ordered work to begin on Tenochtitlán's great pyramid and temple complex.

Acamapichtli was succeeded by his son, Huitzilhuitl. Rulership was not hereditary, but the possible candidates were chosen from a narrow group with noble bloodlines. Huitzilihuitl was very young to take such a prominent position as the tlatoani of an altepetl, but by all accounts he ruled wisely and well, strengthening his city's position by marrying the daughter of the Tepanec emperor, Tezozomoc. This had the effect of greatly reducing the burden of tribute placed upon Tenochtitlán, probably to ensure that the grandsons of the emperor were kept in suitable status.

Conflict between the Tepanec rulers and the Acolhua placed Huitzilihuitl in a difficult position. He was required

to support his overlords in their war but was friendly to the city of Texcoco and its allies. Tenochtitlán maintained an awkward neutrality for as long as possible, which had economic benefits. With existing trade routes disrupted by the war, Tenochtitlán was able to exploit the situation to become an important commercial nexus.

Huitzilihuitl died during the conflict, and his son Chimalpopoca was selected as his replacement. Chimalpopoca was very young – some sources say he was around 12 years old – at the time and might not have been selected had his bloodline not been so strong. But he was the grandson of the Tepanec emperor and related to the much-revered Toltecs, so Tenochtitlán gained a boy king. Huitzilihuitl's previously neutral stance was gradually eroded, until eventually warriors from Tenochtitlán were sent to join the attack on Texcoco.

Texcoco was defeated and the power of the Acolhua broken, leaving the Tepaneca as overlords of the Valley of Mexico. The Acolhua king, Ixtlilxochitl, was killed but his son Nezahualcoyotl survived and was given refuge in Tenochtitlán, possibly with the blessing of Tezozomoc. The city gained further in power as a result of its involvement in the defeat of the Acolhua and was granted permission to build an aqueduct to bring water from springs above Lake Texcoco.

In 1426, the Tepanec emperor Tezozomoc died and was replaced by his son Tayatzin, who died soon afterwards. This was almost certainly the doing of his brother Maxtla, who was not satisfied with his share of the emperor's legacy. This

ABOVE: It is likely that Itzcoatl was behind the assassination of the tlatoani, Chimalpopoca. The act may have been carried out for noble reasons but nevertheless secured the throne for the former advisor and war leader.

9ª guerra de Azcaputzalco

ABOVE: An illustration from the 16th-Century Tovar Codex, depicting warriors storming Azcapotzalco. The city's priests make sacrifices in the hope of turning the tide of battle, whilst the population plead for mercy.

placed Tenochtitlán in a difficult position, as Chimalpopoca had declared support for Tayatzin.

Among the half-brothers of Chimalpopoca was Tlacaelel. Tlacaelel's mother was a commoner or a concubine rather than a noblewoman, but he was ambitious and had the support of his uncle Itzcoatl, who was at the time tlacochcalcatl, or war leader, of Tenochtitlán. Itzcoatl moved to the position of cihuacoatl, chief advisor to the tlatoani, allowing Tlacaelel to take over as war leader.

Chimalpopoca died suddenly, in mysterious circumstances. The obvious suspect was Maxtla, who was widely believed to have poisoned his brother to become Tepanec emperor and also to have made attempts on other leaders including the tlatoani of Tlatelolco. It is possible that this was instead an internal plot, probably on the part of Itzcoatl, since Chimalpopoca was not a wise or well-respected ruler and Tenochtitlán faced a crisis requiring delicate and astute leadership.

In 1428, Itzcoatl was appointed as tlatoani, supported by his nephew Tlacaelel, who advocated war against the Tepanec overlords. Most of Tenochtitlán's elite disagreed, and eventually a delegation was sent to Maxtla. It is claimed that Tlacaelel led this expedition or even went alone, although there is an element of glorification about accounts of his life, which suggests he may not have done everything he was credited with.

According to the story, Tlacaelel marched into the Tepanec capital at Azcapotzalco and demanded to see the emperor. He then delivered an impassioned harangue that impressed Maxtla so much that he did not resort to his usual treachery. After pondering the issue, Maxtla declined the bold demands made by Tlacaelel, who then delivered a formal declaration of war and fought his way out of the Tepanec capital past a group of guards who tried to detain him.

The war went badly for Maxtla, who faced not only Tenochtitlán's warriors but also their allies from other cities and Nezahualcoyotl's forces, who wished to liberate their home city of Texcoco. The defection of Tlacopan to the Tenochtitlán cause brought additional forces to bear, and the Tepanec capital was soon overrun. Azcapotzalco was sacked, with great destruction; although it regained some of its previous status, it was never again a major player in the region's politics.

As cihuacoatl, or senior advisor to the tlatoani, Tlacaelel took charge of mopping up the forces of the defeated Tepaneca and establishing Tenochtitlán as the new centre of power. His role as war leader was taken by Moctezuma Ilhuicamina, as he played an increasingly political role. Among the reforms Tlacaelel instituted was the elevation of Huitzilopochtli to pre-eminence among the gods of his people. He also fostered the belief that the Mexica of Tenochtitlán were better than everyone else and were destined to rule the Valley of Mexico.

Tlacaelel consolidated the power of the ruling family, eroding the traditional privileges of the lesser governing classes; the elders and district leaders who had previously been consulted

BELOW: The merchant class stood a little above most other commoners, and sometimes interacted with the nobility. Some merchants served the king and nobility exclusively, and didn't deal with the general populace.

over matters as diverse as the appointment of a tlatoani and property disputes. Replacing them was a new class of minor nobility composed of warriors rewarded for their service. This not only created a social group grateful to Tlacaelel but moved Tenochtitlán towards becoming a warrior society.

Tlacaelel never ruled Tenochtitlán as its tlatoani. He supported Itzcoatl until his death in 1440, and reputedly declined an invitation to replace him. Instead he remained as chief advisor to Moctezuma Ilhuicamina. The two formed an effective partnership, cementing control of the Triple Alliance over the Valley of Mexico and even launching military expeditions beyond it. By the time of Tlacaelel's death in 1487, Tenochtitlán was the first among near-equals of the Triple Alliance and de facto capital of the Aztec Empire.

## POLITICS AND SOCIETY IN THE AZTEC EMPIRE

The Aztec empire was an overlay rather than a replacement for the local rulership of city-states. Unless there was a reason to depose (and sacrifice) the rulers of a subjugated altepetl, the local elite were left in place but required to provide varying degrees of tribute at intervals. This minimized disruption, although it could have created the possibility of revolt under popular local rulers.

As a result of its political structure, the Aztec empire

was not geographically continuous. The territory of the city-states it ruled was interspersed with unclaimed areas that lay beyond the resources of the local altepetls to annex. A centrally controlled empire might have chosen to integrate these areas, but the Aztec civilization was not inclined to do so. A troublesome area might be aggressively pacified, but the Aztecs had little interest in what lay beyond easy reach of their cities.

Society was stratified, with the ruling family at the top supported by a noble class that supplied leaders, priests and military professionals. Below them was a large common class of tradesmen, merchants and farmers. Male and female roles were clearly divided, with boys receiving some instruction in how to handle weapons and generally a better education than girls. However, as with many societies, there was an unofficial body of 'women's knowledge', which was passed on in addition to the more obvious domestic crafts.

The main social subdivision was the calpulli, which translates as 'big house' but might be thought of as meaning 'extended household'. A calpulli was largely self-contained, with its own leaders, crafters and farmers, and would own land in common among its residents. Usually the majority of people within a calpulli were related to at least some of the others, but in some cases a calpulli might be made up of unrelated people grouped together due to a common trade, connection with a city of origin or ethnic association.

The calpulli system created something between a greatly extended family and a political sub-unit within a city, with the

ABOVE: Slavery was an important part of Aztec society, but unlike many other cultures the status was not hereditary. Slaves were outside the community life of the calpulli but their free children might join one.

# CRIME AND PUNISHMENT

MOST JUSTICE WITHIN THE Aztec empire was swift and harsh. Minor offences might result in humiliation such as public head shaving or the destruction of property, or the offender might be compelled to make restitution for their actions. For more serious crimes, an offender could expect to be put to death in one of various unpleasant ways. Stoning was common, as was strangulation or ritual sacrifice.

Most offences were dealt with by local courts, but very serious crimes, or incidents in which the offender was a noble, were tried by expert judges in Tenochtitlán. Nobles might be personally judged by the emperor at his palace, but on the other hand they could expect harsher sentences for the same crimes. With no prison system, justice in the Aztec empire had to be dealt with quickly. However, in some cases an individual might be exiled instead of receiving other punishments, enslavement was used to both punish a criminal and provide restitution to their victims.

ABOVE: A rebel leader is brought before the court and informed of how he is to be put to death.

leaders of each calpulli having a say in the wider affairs of their home altepetl. In Tenochtitlán, there were eight calpullis within each of the four quarters of the city. In a rural area, a village might be effectively a single calpulli.

The calpulli was more than a social subdivision. Each had a responsibility to pay taxes, which were borne by the calpulli as a whole rather than by individual households. When military forces were raised, men from the same calpulli were grouped into a unit. Since each calpulli was required to provide basic training to its male citizens, the system produced ready-made units of men who had trained together and shared a common identity.

> Slaves did have certain rights and protections, including the ability to buy their freedom, but theirs was a precarious existence.

Records are patchy, but it appears that each calpulli was represented by a single official appointed by its citizens, who was advised by a council of elders. These people, although not nobles, had considerable influence before the reforms of Tlacaelel and retained some power even afterwards.

## SERFS AND SLAVES

Below the commoners were serfs, who worked the land of the noble class and were not part of the calpulli system, and slaves. Slaves did have certain rights and protections, including the ability to buy their freedom, but theirs was a precarious existence. A serf could be enslaved for failing to work hard enough, and a commoner might be sold into slavery to pay off a debt or made a slave as a punishment for certain crimes.

Captives taken in war, whether warriors or a subjugated population, were another source of slaves. Skilled workers were more likely to be retained as slaves than sacrificed, although the fate of any given captive depended largely upon the needs of the priests. If there was a need for large numbers of sacrifices to celebrate an important event or to ask favours from the gods then any captive might face a grim fate. At other times, a larger proportion of those taken in war might be spared.

Slaves in Aztec society were able to own property – including

## CURRENCY AND COUNTERFEIT CACAO

MOST TRADE WAS BY way of barter, but two goods were used as a standard by which to judge the value of others. Quachtli were large white cotton cloaks, whose value varied somewhat according to their quality. The income of a typical commoner equated to around 20 quachtli per year.

Finer comparisons could be made with cacao beans, though again the value of a given bean varied with size and quality.

From records made by the Spanish it appears that quachtli were worth anything from 65 to 300 cacao beans. Beans could be used in the manner of coins in the market, allowing people to make incidental purchases where barter was not appropriate. However, they were sometimes counterfeited using wax or dough, or by hollowing out the bean and replacing the contents with worthless material.

slaves of their own – and might be promoted to high office if they were talented enough. Their children were free; slavery extended only to the person who was enslaved, and not to future generations. A slave had to consent to being sold, with the exception of those who had been judged as incorrigible by the authorities. This was usually on the grounds of being disobedient, surly or making repeated attempts to escape.

Escape was a viable option, since attempting to prevent the escape of another family's slave was punishable by being enslaved. The reasoning behind this law is unclear, but a slave who managed to reach the city ruler's palace or who fulfilled other semi-ritualized conditions could expect to be freed. Similarly, slaves who proved that they had been mistreated, or who had borne children to their masters, were freed.

### ECONOMY AND TRADE

The foundation of the Aztec economy was agriculture; without adequate food supplies no other activity would be possible. In addition to chinampas and conventional fields, communities had small gardens where vegetables were grown. Flowers were also widely planted. The Aztecs understood crop rotation and fertilization, and were able to extract high yields from the land available.

Maize and vegetables formed the basic diet of most citizens, with a little meat. Most of this came from domesticated turkeys or was hunted outside the cities. Farmers also produced cotton and cacao, which were traded widely and used as a measure of value if not a currency as such. Luxury goods such as feathers, art pieces and high-quality clothing were produced by expert craftspeople, while slaves were bought and sold in the marketplaces of the cities.

A city might have many small marketplaces, but the central one in the ceremonial district was by far the most important. Here, goods brought by traders from distant cities were sold alongside the best that local craftspeople could produce. According to Spanish chroniclers, the market at Tlatelolco was

BELOW: A modern interpretation of daily life in Tenochtitlán, from a mural by Diego Riviera. As the citizens go about their business in the marketplace, all their activities are overshadowed by the great temple.

the greatest in the whole Aztec empire, with up to 60,000 people trading there each day.

Traders were well respected in Aztec society, forming a top echelon of the common class, just below the minor nobility in status. Some traders specialized in direct buying and selling to the people of a city; essentially, they were shopkeepers or market traders. Others dealt in bulk goods, while a specialist group known as pochteca moved goods between the cities. Those who did so on behalf of the nobility had a higher status than those who traded in their own right.

Each city had a trade guild, connected to the others by river transport or convoys of porters guarded by warriors. Depots were built to facilitate the movement of goods between the cities, with agents placed in distant areas off the main trade routes. The network allowed goods to flow quickly and freely around the empire, and also served as a conduit for information. Much of this was mundane and overt, but merchants did act as intelligence operatives alongside their normal duties.

The trade network was one of the pillars of the Aztec empire. It ensured that citizens could get what they wanted in the local markets, contributing to their contentment and therefore the stability and economic well-being of the empire. While the flow

## ROCK DUNG

THE AZTECS HARVESTED ALGAE from the lakes near their homes, naming it tecuitlatl, which translates as 'rock dung'. Although unappetizing in its raw form, tecuitlatl was formed into blocks or incorporated into other dishes as a rich protein source. This was particularly important in the Valley of Mexico, as animal-based protein was in short supply. Now named spirulina, the same blue-green algae is in use today as a fertilizer as well as a food supplement. It has been labelled a 'superfood' and, in some quarters at least, attributed the usual near-magical qualities making it capable of solving all manner of weight loss and chronic illness problems. Although some of these claims are questionable, tecuitlatl has proven to be a useful food source in a land where conventional agriculture was problematic.

ABOVE: The bow, named tlahuitolli, was used by some Aztec warriors. Arrows were tipped with flint or obsidian rather than metal, but were no less lethal. Turkey feathers were used for fletching.

of information meant that rulers were well informed of distant events and could react in a timely fashion.

## AZTEC WARFARE

Warfare and conflict were integral to the Aztec way of life. Each of the calpulli within a city was expected to provide training to its male citizens, and to supply warriors when required. Even after the Triple Alliance had become dominant, the city-states of the Valley of Mexico were still prone to outbreaks of violence. Revolts, disputes between the various altepetl, dynastic squabbles and territorial clashes flared up and died down again on a frequent, if irregular, basis.

There was no standing army as such, although a segment of the nobility had military duties and could be considered professional warriors. When a force was required, the bulk of its manpower came from contingents sent by the calpulli, in units of

ABOVE: The macuahuitl
was used by several
Mesoamerican societies,
and many designs existed.
Since the Aztecs preferred
to inflict disabling rather
than fatal injuries, their
weapons usually had
spaced 'blades' of obsidian
rather than a continuous
cutting edge.

400 men. They were protected by shields and sometimes armour of quilted cotton, perhaps augmented with a wooden breastplate. Some warriors wore leather head protection or badges of rank in the form of decorative feathered headdresses. Armament was similar to other Mesoamerican cultures, and included light darts and heavier javelins, both of which were projected using an atlatl. Close-quarters weapons included spears and clubs as well as obsidian-edged sword-clubs, or macuahuitl.

The elite of the army was its Jaguar and Eagle warriors. The Eagle warriors were primarily scouts, who led the march and protected the flanks. Jaguar warriors were the most effective in direct combat; entry to these groups required a warrior to have

RIGHT: The Jaguar and Eagle warriors were the elite of the Aztec military, serving the critical functions of scouts and shock troops respectively. Status was gained through taking captives, so warriors preferred to wound rather than kill their opponents.

# CORN OR MAIZE?

THE TERMS 'CORN' AND 'maize' are often used interchangeably in regard to the Aztecs' staple crop. Both are applicable, but 'maize' is more precise. The term 'corn' is generic and refers to any of the staple cereal crops grown worldwide. In the Valley of Mexico, the staple crop was maize, so a local resident would probably be referring to maize when using the word 'corn'. A Scottish person talking about corn would more likely be referring to barley; for a Ukrainian farmer, 'corn' would be wheat.

In the modern world, the distinction is less important, as cereal crops are less regionalized than in the past. Different types of corn are grown for their specific characteristics, often in the traditional growing area of another type of cereal, but in the Aztec world corn and maize were exactly the same thing.

proved himself several times over in battle. Those who gained membership might continue to rise and someday join the nobility.

The Aztec military also contained a formation known as Otomi, who may have been a super-elite formed from the Jaguar and Eagle warriors or perhaps a sort of Foreign Legion serving the Aztec emperors. The Cuachicqueh, or 'shorn ones' was a unit formed of those who had displayed great prowess and courage many times over. They dressed differently to other warriors, and shaved their heads except for a single braid at the back.

The army was supported by a train of porters, typically youths too young to yet be warriors, who carried supplies provided along with troops by the calpulli. It was usually preceded by spies and then scouts, and by diplomats who attempted to negotiate a surrender or peace deal before fighting began. If they failed, Aztec warfare was typically a vigorous but not particularly well-coordinated affair. Leadership was heroic, in that the king or war leader, and senior commanders, led from the front and were expected to set an example.

A battle typically began with both sides positioned as advantageously as possible, but at this point planning was abandoned in favour of individual prowess. Volleys of javelins and darts preceded a headlong charge with hand weapons, at which point the fighting was more or less an individual matter. Ideally, defeated enemies were not killed but wounded or forced to surrender, which provided sacrifices for the temples and proof of a warrior's prowess in combat.

Wars were fought for the usual political reasons, or to permit a new king to demonstrate his prowess and courage. On many occasions there was no need for a war but one was fought in order to obtain sacrifices. Named xochiyaoyotl, or 'flower war', a campaign of this sort might be fought by mutual agreement, although some cities were almost routinely attacked whenever their more powerful neighbours needed sacrifices.

The flower war was a limited conflict, aimed not at regime change or subjugating the enemy – at least, not directly – but at fulfilling a religious need. Of course, it could be used as a political gambit by a city-state ruler who wanted to intimidate his neighbours, or as a broad hint to possible rebels of the fate that awaited them. Thus, the flower wars were not entirely divorced from politics, but certainly had a different aim to most European conflicts of the era.

## AZTEC RELIGION AND HUMAN SACRIFICE

The Aztec cosmos consisted of an underworld with nine layers and a celestial realm of thirteen, separated by the mundane world. The great temple at Tenochtitlán was the centre of the world and the meeting point of the other realms. Everything moved in cycles, ending in destruction and rebirth, and how a person died dictated what happened to them after death.

LEFT: Tlaloc, who brought rain and therefore the crops that fed the Aztec people, is very similar to the Maya god Chac. Sacrifices to him were made in the hope of 'good rain' that would nourish the crops rather than causing floods and destruction.

Those who earned the honour of being sacrificed to Huitzilopochtli would fight alongside the gods to save the universe, but most people could expect to have to pass through the underworld and eventually be reincarnated. Their spirits might have to wander the world for a time, and not everyone came back as a human. Some spirits would eventually return as creatures such as birds.

The Aztec empire absorbed many gods along with the population of the city-states that worshipped them. More than 200 have been identified, although some may be aspects of a different form of another god worshipped elsewhere. The Aztecs believed that their era was the 'Fifth Sun'; the fifth era in a cycle of creation, life and destruction. Each Sun was ruled over by a different god, and was brought to an end by an act of sacrifice and renewal.

Chief among the Aztec gods was Huitzilopotchtli, a god of war. According to legend, Huitzilopotchtli led the ancestors of the Aztecs to their new home at Tenochtitlán, although he may not have been their chief god at the time of the migration. The emperor Tlacaelel elevated Huitzilopotchtli to pre-eminent

OPPOSITE: God of the sun and of warfare, Huitzilopochtli was foremost among the Aztec deities. His name translates as Hummingbird of the South or Hummingbird of the Left, in keeping with the Aztec association between warriors and hummingbirds.

status alongside Tlaloc; before this, he was worshipped as a god of the hunt. This transition from hunter to warrior and leader may represent a change in the world view of the Mexica people; they had changed from nomadic hunter-gatherers to a powerful, organized state wielding great military power.

Huitzilopotchtli was the son of Coatlicue, goddess of life and death. Coatlicue became pregnant by way of a ball of feathers she encountered at the temple on Coatepec (Snake Hill), which angered her daughter Coyolxauhqui, goddess of the moon. Along with her 400 brothers (the stars of the Milky Way), Coyolxauhqui went to kill their mother. Although unable to prevent his mother from being decapitated, Huitzilopotchtli sprang from her womb ready for war and slew Coyolxauhqui and all her brothers, hurling the moon-goddess's body down the mountain.

Huitzilopotchtli is often represented as an eagle or a hummingbird. Aztec warriors were associated with hummingbirds, adorning themselves as did the nobility with brightly coloured feathers. In addition to warfare, Huitzilopotchtli presided over human sacrifice. Warriors were particularly favoured, and were flung down the temple steps after having their hearts ripped out in an echo of Huitzilopotchtli's great victory over his siblings.

Rain was another important aspect of Aztec life, and the chief rain god Tlaloc was a near-equal of Huitzilopotchtli. Tlaloc appears to be one of the gods the Aztecs inherited or co-opted from the Olmecs and the Teotihuacan civilization. Tlaloc's favour was necessary for agriculture; his main festival took place at the end of the dry season around the beginning of April. Children were considered particularly pleasing sacrifices to Tlaloc.

Quetzalcóatl, the 'feathered serpent', is the most widely known Aztec god today. Quetzalcóatl was worshipped, sometimes under other names, by the Maya, the Toltecs and other Mesoamerican civilizations. He was a benefactor of

> Aztec warriors were associated with hummingbirds, adorning themselves as did the nobility with brightly coloured feathers.

OPPOSITE: The most widely-known Aztec god is Quetzalcóatl, the feathered serpent. Originally worshipped as a fertility deity with power over food crops, by the Aztec era Quetzalcóatl was associated with death and rebirth, and was revered as a patron of priests and goldsmiths.

humanity, who provided maize and taught people how to farm it. It was long believed that the legend of Quetzalcóatl, who promised to return to humanity someday, was a factor in the collapse of the Aztec empire. The story goes that the light-skinned Cortés and his men were mistaken for the returning Quetzalcóatl. This is now generally considered to be an invention of the Spanish after they conquered the Aztec empire.

Tezcatlipoca was a god of night and darkness, brother to Quetzalcóatl and often his enemy. Their conflict also occurs in Toltec mythology and may be a reflection of internal conflicts in the city of Tollan. Tezcatlipoca was important to Aztec rulers as the embodiment of law, or at least the punishment of wrongdoing. He was associated with obsidian and was known as the Lord of the Smoking Mirror.

The other gods of the Aztecs were associated with one of three functions: war and sacrifice; rain and fertility or agriculture; and the heavens. Tonatiuh was the present sun god, created by the self-sacrifice of the minor god Nanahuatzin. His role was complex: on the one hand, he was the nurturing source of light and warmth; on the other, a demanding warrior who required endless sacrifices to prevent the light of the universe from going out.

## THE FIVE SUNS

THE FIRST SUN BEGAN with the creation of the universe by the sons of Tonacacihuatl and Tonacatecuhtli, who were male and female aspects of the god Ometeotl. The sons created a complete universe and peopled it with gods and humans. They realized that humans needed fire to survive, but to bring it to humanity a god had to sacrifice himself. Tezcatlipoca did so, beginning the First Sun.

The people of the First Sun were giants, but they were killed and eaten by jaguars that may have been aspects of Tezcatlipoca, who was angry at being displaced by the other gods. The Second Sun was ruled over by Quetzalcóatl, and its people were humans. This Sun came to an end when Tezcatlipoca challenged Quetzalcóatl and overthrew him. Hurricanes destroyed most of the world and the surviving humans were turned into monkeys.

Tlaloc ruled during the Third Sun but was undone by Quetzalcóatl, who used a rain of fire against him. The surviving humans were again transformed, this time into turkeys and butterflies. Chalchiuhtlicue, wife of Tlaloc, ruled this Sun but humanity was again destroyed, this time by a great flood. The survivors became fish.

The gods then debated which of them would be sacrificed to start a new Sun. While they argued, the minor god Nanahuatzin jumped into the sacrificial fire, and Tecuciztecatl went after him. This resulted in two suns, which would have destroyed the world. The gods solved this problem by hurling a rabbit at

The Aztecs used the Mesoamerican calendar, with its 52-year cycle, and feared that the light would not return at the end of each cycle. They held a New Fire Ceremony at midnight on the last day of the cycle, hoping to keep their gods strong by great sacrifices and thus ensure the sun would rise on a new cycle in the morning.

## EMPERORS OF THE AZTECS

Terms such as 'king' and 'emperor' do not entirely fit the political situation in Mesoamerica, at least not in the context of their European meaning. The Aztec empire was more of a confederation, with the rulers of the main city-states exerting varying degrees of control over other cities. Nevertheless, by the late 1400s, the region was dominated by the Triple Alliance and the ruler of Tenochtitlán was the foremost of its leaders. Although his power was not absolute, the tlatoani of

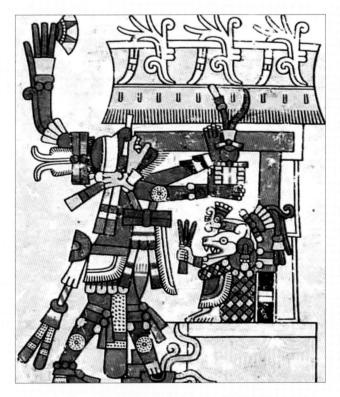

Tecuciztecatl, reducing his brightness so that he became the moon.

There were no people to fill this new world, since everyone had been killed by the flood or turned into fish. Quetzalcóatl solved this problem by stealing the bones of the dead from the underworld and sprinkling them with his blood. With help from the other gods, he brought humanity back to life. This was the origin of the practice of bloodletting, honouring the gods and thanking them for the gift of life.

LEFT: Tezcatlipoca was associated with the night sky and the constellation of Ursa Major. He had numerous aspects, as a patron of warriors and kings as well as magic.

Tenochtitlán could wield the military forces of the whole region and subjugate those who opposed his will.

Moctezuma Ilhuicamina, known as Moctezuma I, ruled from 1440 to 1469. He inherited a powerful state from his predecessor and uncle, Itzcoatl, but soon faced challenges in the form of a severe drought and war with Chalco. A successful campaign was followed by conquests stretching all the way to the Gulf coast. The former Zapotec city of Mitla in the Oaxaca valley was captured and garrisoned around 1450, and in 1458 the Aztecs began making war on the Mixtec people.

The campaign was a success, although it appears that no attempt was made to subjugate the Mixtec people. Some leaders were executed or sacrificed and tribute requirements put in place, but the Aztec forces departed without imposing lasting changes on the region. By the time of Moctezuma I's death in 1469, he had expanded the Aztec empire beyond the Valley of

BELOW: Moctezuma I expanded the Aztec empire to even greater extents, but in so doing perhaps sowed the seeds of its downfall. Controlling such a large area was made more difficult by the cultural differences between the Aztecs and their new subject people outside the Valley of Mexico.

Mexico and established the classic form of Aztec society.

Moctezuma I was succeeded by Axayacatl, who continued to expand the empire. He was very young to be emperor, probably only 19 at the time of his coronation, but already a proven warrior. He launched a 'flower war' against Cotaxtla, which was in rebellion at the time, and obtained large numbers of sacrifices for his coronation. More military success followed, though Axayacatl was wounded in combat with warriors from Toluca.

Concerned about the economic power of Tlatelolco, which could have been used to undermine his own position, Axayacatl decided to subjugate the city. The ostensible reason for the conflict was the mistreatment of Axayacatl's sister, who was married to the tlatoani of Tlatelolco, but the goal was conquest and the elimination of any threat. The war was declared in the traditional manner, with emissaries from Tenochtitlán declaring their intentions and providing weapons to the enemy.

ABOVE: Axayacatl's military prowess meant that he was chosen to ascend the throne, much to the displeasure of his two older brothers Tizoc and Ahuitzotl.

With the conflict thus legitimized, Axayacatl faced a prepared and powerful enemy. To do otherwise would be dishonourable and displeasing to the gods as well as gaining Axayacatl a reputation for treachery. This openness about conflict and lack of guile in carrying it out suited the Aztec way of life, but it would prove to be a liability against the Spanish a few years later.

Axayacatl's forces were victorious, succeeding in cornering Moquihuix, ruler of Tlatelolco, and his followers atop their city's great pyramid. From there they were flung to their deaths in a manner pleasing to Huitzilopochtli. Despite this good omen, a campaign in 1478 against the Tarascans ended in disaster and the loss of nearly 20,000 warriors.

ABOVE: **Although carvings depict great achievements and conquests, Tizoc was a poor strategist who lost large numbers of warriors due to elementary mistakes. His rule was characterized by revolts and defeats in battle.**

Axayacatl ordered the final phase of building on the great temple at Tenochtitlán and, despite his setbacks, was lord of a stable and powerful empire when he died, aged just 30, around 1481. He was succeeded by his brother, Tizoc, whose reign was short and disastrous.

A nephew of Itzcoatl, Tizoc came from a good bloodline but had already established himself as a lacklustre commander as war leader under Axayacatl. He was expected to launch a military campaign as soon as he became emperor, to obtain sacrifices and demonstrate his worthiness. Tizoc's chosen target was the region around Ixmiquilpan and Metztitlán, whose defenders should have been easy prey. However, Tizoc chose to give battle in a narrow valley instead of the customary plain.

The traditional Aztec mode of warfare was straightforward, substituting numbers and enthusiasm for clever manoeuvres and stratagems. On a narrow frontage, Tizoc's force could not take advantage of its superiority in numbers and suffered heavy casualties against well-positioned and desperate defenders. Tizoc's return with only a handful of sacrifices to celebrate his coronation convinced Tizoc's subordinates that he was a weak and incompetent ruler, an impression borne out in subsequent campaigns.

Rebellions broke out, and city-states refused to pay their tribute or sent reduced amounts. Tizoc had to respond, but mishandled the campaigns and suffered further defeats. Lacking the confidence of his own supporters, let alone the obedience of the distant city-states, Tizoc's reign spiralled downwards until he was poisoned in 1486.

Tizoc was succeeded by his brother, Ahuitzotl, who was altogether more forceful and competent. Ahuitzotl appears to have been a warrior by nature, preferring to camp with his troops rather than take over the palaces of his conquests. Those conquests were many, gained by traditional Aztec vigour on the battlefield aided by a gift for strategy that went beyond the straightforward.

Ahuitzotl undid the damage done by his brother's weak reign and made the point that he was a different sort of ruler with the largest human sacrifice ever seen. Up to 20,000 captives were sacrificed, many by Ahuitzotl personally, atop his new temple at Tenochtitlán. Some accounts place the lines of captives waiting to be slain at over 5km (3 miles) long. Naturally, those of his recent enemies not taking part were invited to watch the festivities.

Ahuitzotl was ruler of an Aztec empire containing 371 city-states. During his reign, Tenochtitlán reached its largest population, requiring the construction of an additional aqueduct. He died suddenly in 1502 or 1503, as a result of an accident during a period of flooding, and was succeeded by his nephew, Moctezuma II.

BELOW: Expansion and rebuilding of the Great Temple at Tenochtitlán went on throughout the Aztec era. This memorial shows Tizoc and his brother Ahuitzotl, who succeeded him, performing a religious ceremony to celebrate another round of improvements.

## THE COLLAPSE OF THE AZTEC EMPIRE

Moctezuma II inherited an enormous empire, but one that was becoming increasingly difficult to control. Expansion beyond the limits of ethnic and cultural affinities meant that subject people on the fringes of the empire were more prone to revolt than those of the Valley of Mexico, especially when expected to provide large numbers of sacrifices. Moctezuma II responded by strengthening the position of the nobility in return for their support, and by harsh measures against his opponents. His coronation was accompanied by a suitably large number of sacrifices garnered among rebels against his rule.

A series of successful campaigns up to 1510 suppressed rebellions and brought new territories into the empire, accompanied by harsh tribute demands and the threat of brutal

## METHODS OF SACRIFICE

TYPICALLY, CAPTURED WARRIORS were slain on an altar atop the sacred pyramid, their heart cut out with an obsidian knife. The body was then decapitated and sometimes flayed of its skin, then hurled down the temple steps. Severed heads may or may not have been placed on display.

This was not the only method of sacrifice. Some captives were shot with arrows or darts, or killed in ritual combat. Accounts vary: in some, the sacrifice was expected to fight to the death against four opponents armed with an inadequate weapon. Other versions were far more dangerous for the priests. In some accounts, the sacrifice was an accomplished warrior armed with a club or mace. His opponents were four priests armed with obsidian-edged sword-clubs designed to rip flesh and spill blood rather than kill quickly. The better

fight the sacrifice put up and the longer it, the more pleasing the incident would be to the gods. It is not known if the sacrifice killing one or more of the priests was considered a bonus.

RIGHT: Although other methods of sacrifice were used, the Aztecs favoured cutting open the chest with an obsidian knife and extracting the still-beating heart of their victims.

suppression if they were not met.
This might have been sufficient
to cement Moctezuma's power
under other circumstances;
he had pleased the nobility
with concessions and still
managed to retain the support
of most commoners. However,
the arrival of the Spanish
in Mesoamerica provided
Moctezuma's enemies with an
alternative to submission.

In 1519, as Moctezuma was
putting down another wave
of rebellions, news came that
a Spanish expedition under
Hernan Cortés had landed
on the Gulf coast. It has
been claimed that the Aztecs
thought Cortés was their god
Quetzalcóatl making his return,
and that they were demoralized
by evil portents, but it is questionable whether this was the case.

Cortés had with him around 500 men and a small number
of horses, which the Aztecs had never seen before. He benefited
from the best and most modern weaponry that Europe could
provide – primitive firearms and light artillery pieces – and
was driven by religious zeal and a desire for riches. Cortés also
benefited from the disaffection of the people he encountered
along the Gulf coast, who were in many cases willing to side with
the newcomers against the emperor in Tenochtitlán. The arrival
of Europeans was also accompanied by outbreaks of disease that
weakened the local city-states and, perhaps more importantly,
upset the social order.

Moctezuma attempted to bribe the Spaniards to leave, which
served only to demonstrate the wealth that was to be had in
the New World. Cortés began building alliances with the local

ABOVE: The empire of
Moctezuma II was not
stable, with rebellions
breaking out as quickly as
they could be put down.
Successful campaigns
garnered large numbers
of sacrifices but this was
not sufficient to protect
the Aztec empire from the
European threat.

ABOVE: **Moctezuma II was forced to be diplomatic towards Cortés, offering hospitality and bribes rather than a first-hand demonstration of Aztec sacrificial practices. Cortés correctly interpreted this as a sign of weakness and exploited the situation for all it was worth.**

tribes, who wanted rid of their Aztec overlords. He dealt with the internal politics of his own expedition by a combination of manipulation and direct action, damaging his ships so that his men had no choice but to fight and win in the coming conflict.

As Cortés and his expedition marched inland they at first benefited from myths of their invincibility and fear of their horses, which they ruthlessly exploited. The illusion was dented by near-defeat at Tlaxcala, but conflict soon turned to alliance. The enemies of the Aztecs could not have predicted the implications of the Europeans' arrival, and saw only an opportunity to further their own agenda.

## THE BEGINNING OF THE END

Cortés and his force were in part a catalyst and in part a facilitator of the Aztec collapse. They made war in a way not usually seen in Mesoamerica, ignoring conventions about formal declaration and limited outcomes. Theirs was not a flower war to win sacrifices; the Spanish fought to subjugate their enemies and did so with every available stratagem in addition to their strange weapons.

Arriving at Tenochtitlán, Cortés and his expedition were greeted in a friendly fashion but correctly suspected a trap. They took Moctezuma II captive, hoping to control his empire through him. This worked for a time, but in 1520, amid an uprising against the Spanish, Moctezuma was killed by his own people, who felt betrayed. The Spaniards were blamed for his death and had to fight their way clear of the city.

Moctezuma II was succeeded by his brother, Cuitláhuac, who had always advocated violent resistance to the Spanish. As many as 100,000 warriors followed Cuitláhuac, who was able to drive out the Spaniards but found he had gained only partial control of an empire in tatters. Rebellions were breaking out in many areas, along with quieter refusals or omissions to pay the expected tribute.

Cuitláhuac reigned for only 80 days before dying in a smallpox epidemic. During that time he achieved limited success, but was unable to reintegrate some of the rebellious cities. It may be that his successes were his undoing; his forces captured numerous potential sacrifices in battle against Tlaxcalteca, which was in alliance with the Spanish. One of them is reputed to have carried smallpox, which spread rapidly throughout Tenochtitlán.

Cuitláhuac was succeeded by Cuauhtémoc, nephew and son-in-law to Moctezuma II. He too had opposed the Spanish from the beginning and is credited with inciting the incident in which his uncle was killed. He rallied enormous support – anything from 200,000 to 500,000 warriors, depending on the source – and fortified Tenochtitlán against the Spanish. The causeway bridges, constructed long ago for just this purpose, were removed to deny access.

BELOW: Although the Spanish were experts at torture, Cuauhtémoc resisted them bravely, refusing to reveal where his city's treasures were hidden. He was eventually executed, never having betrayed his people, and with him the Aztec empire came to an end.

Now reinforced with additional troops, the Spanish built ships to assault Tenochtitlán, and in the meantime they ravaged the nearby towns and cities. Cuauhtémoc led expeditions against them but could not prevail against cannon and cavalry. Forced back into his capital, he led a campaign of urban guerrilla warfare, which the Spanish countered by systematically destroying every building they were able to reach. Cuauhtémoc's forces were confined in an ever-diminishing perimeter and eventually were unable to prevent the Spanish establishing a bridgehead on the island.

Starving and depleted by disease, the Aztecs held out until Cuauhtémoc was captured. After a brief period of civility in which he was offered the chance to keep his throne if he became a Spanish vassal – an offer that Cuauhtémoc would have well understood – he was tortured in the hope that he would reveal the location of his city's treasure. Defiant to the

BELOW: The fall of Tenochtitlán in 1521 was an indication that the Aztec empire's power had been broken by the Europeans. Some continued resistance took place, but the heart of the empire had been cut out.

last, Cuauhtémoc refused to cooperate and even attempted to coordinate a rebellion. He was eventually executed to prevent him from leading an uprising.

Tenochtitlán surrendered to the Spanish in August 1521, and its last emperor was executed in 1525 while accompanying Cortés and his entourage on an expedition to Honduras. His war leader, Tlacotzin, was to have succeeded him, but did not live long enough to reach Tenochtitlán. By this time, the fabric of the Aztec empire had completely unravelled. The social structure that had permitted its unique culture to flourish and create an effective, vigorous, not-quite empire was gone.

## THE END OF INDIGENOUS CIVILIZATION IN MESOAMERICA

Even if the Spanish had returned home or been driven out, the Aztec empire was gone forever. A new Mesoamerican civilization might have arisen in time, but the conquerors had no intention of leaving. Instead, they consolidated their control over the region and overlaid their culture on its people. Conversion to Christianity swept away the old gods, with palaces for the new rulers and cathedrals to their god built from the stone of ancient pyramids.

Mesoamerica now had regular contact with Europe. This brought plunder and disease, and the wanton looting of ancient treasures. Less obviously, it brought to an end the millennia of isolation that had led to the rise of such a unique culture. Yet this was not a one-way process. Mesoamerica was changed by the influx of foreign conquerors and opportunists, but its values and ideas were not discarded and replaced. Today's Central American nations have much in common with those in Europe, but much that is their own. Indeed, it could be said that one unique culture was destroyed but another rose in its place.

And in the jungles of the Panama Isthmus, the highlands of old Mesoamerica and even in the middle of modern cities, the carvings, statues and pyramids of the ancient civilizations still survive. Much still waits to be learned about these cultures, and they remain among the most intriguing mysteries of our world.

# BIBLIOGRAPHY

Bernand, Carmen: *The Incas: People of the Sun* (Abrams Books, 1994)

Bruhns, Karen Olsen: *Ancient South America* (Cambridge University Press, 1994)

Carrasco, David: *City of Sacrifice: The Aztec Empire and the Role of Violence in Civilisation* (Beacon Press, 2000)

Carrasco, David: *Religions of Mesoamerica* (Waveland Press, 2013)

Coe, Michael D and Houston, Stephen D: *The Maya* (Thames and Hudson, 2015)

Clendinnen, Inga: *Aztecs: An Interpretation* (Cambridge University Press, 1991)

D'Altroy, Terence N: *The Incas* (Wiley-Blackwell, 2014)

Davies, Nigel: *The Toltecs: Until the Fall of Tula* (University of Oklahoma Press, 1978)

Deihl, Richard A: *Tula: The Toltec Capital of Ancient Mexico* (Thames and Hudson, 1983)

Deihl, Richard: *The Olmecs: America's First Civilisation* (Thames and Hudson, 2004)

Flannery, V Kent and Marcus, Joyce (Editors): *The Cloud People: Divergent Evolution of the Zapotec and Mixtec Civilisations* (Eliot Werner Publications; Percheron Press, 2003)

MacQuarrie, Kim: *Last Days of the Incas* (Simon & Schuster, 2008)

Miguel Leon-Portilla, Miguel: *The Broken Spears: The Aztec Account of the Conquest of Mexico* (Beacon Press, 2006)

Mithen, Steven: *After the Ice: A Global Human History 20000–5000BC* (Harvard University Press, 2006)

Morris, Craig and von Hagen, Adrian: *The Incas* (Thames & Hudson, 2012)

Philips, Charles: *The Complete Illustrated History of the Aztec & Maya: The Definitive Chronicle of the Ancient Peoples of Central America and Mexico – Including the Aztec, Olmec, Mixtec, Toltec and Zapotec.* (Hermes House, 2015)

Robb, Matthew (Editor): *Teotihuacan: City of Water, City of Fire* (University of California Press, 2017)

Rosenwig, M Robert: *The Beginnings of Mesoamerican Civilisation: Inter-regional Interaction and the Olmec* (Cambridge University Press, 2009)

Sharer, Robert J & Traxler, Loa P: *The Ancient Maya* (Stanford University Press, 2005)

Taube, Karl: *Aztec and Maya Myths* (University of Texas Press, 1993)

Townsend, Richard F: *The Aztecs* (Thames & Hudson, 2009)

Various Contributors: *The Mayas of the Classic Period* (Antique Collectors' Club, 1999)

Various Contributors: *The Aztec Empire* (Guggenheim Museum, 2004)

# INDEX

# PICTURE CREDITS

**Alamy:** 10 (Neil Bowman), 12 (RGB Ventures/ Superstock), 13 (North Wind Picture Archive), 14 (Stocktrek Images/Roman Garcia Mora), 15 (Chico Sanchez), 18 (Simon Curtis), 28 (Ricardo Ribas), 30 (Reciprocity Images Editorial), 32 (Peter Horree), 37 (Sergi Reboredo), 39 (Deco), 41 (Peter Horree), 42 (Robert Fried), 44 (Interfoto), 46 top (Peter Horree), 46 bottom (Martin Norris Travel Photography), 49 (Vario Images/ McPhoto), 52 (Barna Tanko), 55 & 56 (Peter Horree), 57 (World History Archive), 58 (Carver Mostardi), 59 (Heritage Image Partnership/ Fine Art Images), 60 (EDU Vision), 66 & 69 (John Mitchell), 72 (Richard Maschmeyer), 75 (The Picture Art Collection), 78 (World History Archive), 79 (AGE Fotostock), 80 (Masterbliss), 82 (dbimages), 83 (John Mitchell), 88 (Travelpix), 90 (AGE Fotostock/Cem Canbay), 93 (Carver Mostardi), 95 (Martyn Vickery), 99 (Chico Sanchez), 100 (Image Broker/Jose Antonio Moreno Castellano), 101 (Maria Victoria Herrera), 102 (Francesco Palerno), 104 (Rob Crandall), 107 (Heritage Image Partnership/ Werner Forman), 110 (World History Archive), 112 (Ajith Achuthan), 116 (Cindy Hopkins), 117 (Stefano Ravera), 118 (Peter Horree), 119 (Anne Lewis), 121 (Sabena Jane Blackbird), 122 (Natalia Lukiianova), 130 (Kavita Favelle), 133 (Sabena Jane Blackbird), 136 (Lordprice Collection), 137 (Prisma Archivo), 138 (Heritage Image Partnership/Werner Forman), 145 (Javier Palmieri), 146 (Adrian Wojcik), 150 (Kseniya Ragozina), 152/153 (National Geographic Creative), 155 (World History Archive), 156 (Atlaspix), 157 (Interfoto), 161 (Sabena Jane Blackbird), 162 (M. Timothy O'Keefe), 164 (Brian Van Tighem), 165 (Heritage Image Partnership/ Fine Art Images), 167 (Chronicle), 168 (Interfoto), 169 & 170 (North Wind Picture Archive), 172 (Bosiljka Zutich), 174 (Mireille Vautier), 177 (Lebrecht Music & Arts), 178 (CPC Collection), 180 (Mireille Vautier), 183 (North Wind Picture Archive), 184 (J. Enrique Molina), 185 (ART Collection), 187 (Science History Images/ Photo Researchers), 188 both (The Picture Art Collection), 189 (Chronicle), 190 (Art Collection 2), 200 top (The Picture Art Collection), 202 (Science History Images/Photo Researchers), 205 (Mireille Vautier), 207 (The History Collection), 208 (The Picture Art Collection), 209 (The History Collection), 212 (North Wind Picture Archive), 213 (bilwissedition), 214 (Science History Images/ Photo Researchers), 215 (The Artchives)

**Alamy/Granger Collection:** 19, 45, 65, 68, 77, 134, 143, 154, 159, 194, 197, 199, 203, 210, 216

**Depositphotos:** 6 (Andrei Orlov), 29 (Jkraft5), 87 (pxhidalgo), 96/97 (pxhidalgo), 106 (Topphoto), 108/109 (Lunamarina), 113 (Somatuscani), 115 (Mari Tere M), 124 (Stylepics), 126/127 (Byelikova), 128 (Filipefrazao), 129 (Pyty), 131 (Salko3p), 132 (Pyty), 141 (Javarman), 142 (Ammmit), 148/149 (Armando Frazao), 175 (Soft_Light 69)

**Dreamstime:** 64 (Enrique Gomez), 70/71 (Raul Garcia Herrera), 73 (Ivan Paunovic)

**Getty Images:** 21 (Corbis), 22 (Image Bank/Javier Pierini), 26 (AFP), 27 (Corbis/George Steinmetz), 40 (Gamma-Rapho/Marc Deville), 47 (Universal Images Group/Universal History Archive), 84 (National Geographic/ Yeorgos Lampathakis), 85 (National Geographic/Kenneth Garrett), 92 (Lonely Planet Images/Brent Winebrenner), 98 (Print Collector), 160 (Gallo Images/Michael Langford), 163 (Fernando Podolski), 173 (Universal Images Group), 193 & 200 bottom (Dorling Kindersley)

**Getty Images/De Agostini:** 8, 11, 35, 50, 53, 67, 89, 103, 176, 182, 192, 211

**Shutterstock:** 16 (Rafal Cichawa), 24 (Lurii Kazakov), 25 & 33 (Christian Vinces), 34 (Canyalcin), 38 (SL-Photography), 62/63 (DR Travel Photo & Video)